MAKE LOVE NOT SCARS

MAKE LOVE NOT SCARS

A STORY OF FIGHTING
BACK AND WINNING

RIA SHARMA

First published by Westland Publications Private Limited in 2019
61, 2nd Floor, Silverline Building, Alapakkam Main Road, Maduravoyal, Chennai 600095

Westland and the Westland logo are the trademarks of Westland Publications Private Limited, or its affiliates.

ISBN: 9789387894785

10 9 8 7 6 5 4 3 2 1

Typeset by SÜRYA, New Delhi

Printed at Thomson Press (India) Ltd

This book is for every girl who wants to change the world but is told that the world is too big.
Remember, you are the world.

This one's for the survivor in all of us and, of course, the survivors themselves.

And you, yes *you*!
You picked up this book and now one more person in the world knows about acid attacks.
Thank you for helping me further my cause.
I am truly in your debt.

Contents

Foreword

FLYING BACK FROM SINGAPORE WHERE I HAD BEEN working the previous two years, I returned to my hometown Leeds in England to take up a position as head of BA Hons Fashion Design and Communication at Leeds Arts University. This is where I met Ria, an international student from New Delhi who had just completed her first year of study and, by all accounts, was not doing well. Her grades were low—borderline failure; and her attendance was poor. Her design skills were weak and she seemed to be disengaged from her studies. Ria stood out as one of the only international students in the department and although there was definitely a perception of privilege about her, I was aware that she faced many challenges including being far away from her home in India which she loved, living in stark cultural contrast in an industrial metropolitan city in the north of England with very different expectations from her.

In her second year of study, Ria was required to make a short piece of film in order to learn the basic techniques of story-telling and editing. In it she featured herself wandering around European city streets in a party dress with a bottle of champagne in one hand and a cigarette in the other. It was deliberately rebellious and controversial. When my colleague Paul showed it to me, my first thought was: Why is she making this film? So I started to question what her motivation was. What reaction did she expect? What was she really trying to say? In that short piece of film I saw a lost young girl, looking for her place in the world, and it became my responsibility to help her find that place.

After a second year of many missed classes and poorly executed papers that she presented with very little thought, Ria entered her third and final year and I became her personal tutor. I asked her how she wanted to remember her time studying in England and she told me she was fed up with not performing. She wanted to do well but she didn't know how. She was not the type of student who could simply apply themselves to their work as instructed in order to receive a grade. That wasn't enough for her.

After some in-depth tutorials where we discussed the relationship between fashion politics and identity, I tried to draw out of her something that would really capture her imagination and allow her to focus on her final year with dedication. She started to explore concepts around women's rights in India and I was fascinated by her ability to tell stories and saw how articulate and passionate she could be when inspired. For her first final year project, she'd made a very unusual conceptual piece of transparent plastic underwear with strips of embroidered cotton running through it with messages of women's suppression. I wasn't at all sure at the time how she was going to execute this idea but she was adamant she could make it work—and I was intrigued. She decided to make another film with this garment when she went to India for the holidays. When she returned, I felt everything had changed. The film was only a couple of minutes long but I was hooked from the first second. Every part of it was considered: the model, the garment, the setting, the soundtrack, the message and, most importantly, the intense emotion.

Ria was now starting to work at the standard I knew she was capable of and I was so excited by what she was going to do next. I had been very strict with her about her previous work because I knew she was capable of more and she was undervaluing herself. If I hadn't seen her potential I would never have been so critical of her and, now, finally, she had produced something exceptional. So when it came to her final major project, I knew I wasn't going to let her slack off for one minute. I was going to challenge her to her limits.

From then on it was like a roller-coaster. For both of us, as she had only a few months left of her degree. There was an online booking system for tutorials which she rarely adhered to. Often if she had an idea she would knock on my office door and say, 'Suzy, I can't wait until next Tuesday. I need to see you now.' It was hard to say no to Ria.

One day she came for a tutorial and showed me a black-and-white photo of a girl who had suffered an acid attack in India. She had seen the story online and it bothered her. A lot. She had come to show it to me. She said that she couldn't stop thinking about the story of this girl and she didn't know what to do. Without taking a breath she talked to me about everything she had discovered, how wrong it was that this was happening and, most importantly, how could she respond to it. She just asked me straight out how she could make this subject fit into her fashion studies as it wasn't fashion. And I said, 'Let's find a way to make it fit.'

So it was decided that day that she would return to India immediately rather than waiting until the holidays to make a documentary highlighting the issue of acid attacks on women. She was so eager to get going by this point that there was no stopping her. She had such a sense of urgency and she was so persistent that she didn't give me the option to say no to anything. I felt compelled to facilitate this, even though the enormity of what I was encouraging her to do made me feel nervous. I certainly didn't have any idea at that point what was going to unfold, but I knew in my heart that this was not just a college project for her. This was a life's work, and I told her so.

I believe established rules matter for everyday structures in life; however, sometimes, controversial and challenging subjects need greater flexibility and more personal consideration, so rules, although good in theory, can sometimes fail a person in practice and this is where I found myself with Ria. What was more important?

Sticking to the online tutorial booking system or allowing her to burst into my office anytime of the day gushing about what she wanted to do and what was possible? It would have been like holding back a wave. So I bent the rules: tutorial times were not adhered to. Travelling to India and not returning because she had decided to visit a survivor at a rehabilitation unit at the last minute became acceptable. Regular Skype tutorials and WhatsApp messages at ad hoc times of the day became our way of communication and, step by step, day by day, I watched Ria create *Make Love Not Scars* first as a documentary, which never actually got made, and then as a registered NGO.

The launch photos that she produced were fantastic. She photographed the survivors with make-up and flowers in their hair. She had the ability to create powerful, uplifting and beautiful images of women struck by such tragedy. It was pure brilliance. *Make Love Not Scars*, an idea to empower the survivors of acid attacks and make them visible in society, was born. I remember looking at the images she sent me from that shoot and feeling a rush of emotion. I was elated and proud of what she had accomplished.

There were times when Ria became overwhelmed by the enormity and severity of what she had undertaken and the huge responsibility. After visiting a rehabilitation unit she messaged me to say she couldn't carry on and was quitting the project. I asked her if she wanted to scale back and return to the UK, but she never took that option and eventually decided to continue. I was unsettled because I knew I had encouraged her to pursue this work and she was now being exposed to so much politically as well as emotionally. However, I also knew her path was set.

Ria returned to LCA to submit her work and completed her studies that spring. She was one of my last graduating students after twenty years of teaching in higher education, and since I worked at LCA only for the two years she was there, it seems as though we were destined to meet. Her final major project was one of the most inspiring, dynamic and sincere assignments that I have ever seen a student produce even though, by this time, she was far too busy to notice.

Over the course of the last few years I have watched with such admiration as she has gone on to work tirelessly on *Make Love Not Scars*, winning many well-deserved awards and accolades and gaining a highly respected international reputation as a social activist. Starting from a small seed in my cramped office in Leeds to building such a powerful force fighting injustice and violence and effecting positive change on a daily basis in women's lives, hers is truly a remarkable and brave journey.

I feel deeply honoured that Ria has asked me to write the foreword to her first book and I am so excited to see how the next stages of her life unfold.

Suzy Mason
Leeds, England, 2018

The smell.

The screams—I could hear them from a mile away. The massive locks on the door were probably to stop the terrified victims from trying to flee their gruesome reality. I was in the burn ward and I knew it was going to be one hell of a ride.

Until that moment, I wanted to believe that it was all a part of my imagination—really, how bad could it be? But as I walked through the door, I knew it was too late—the doors were locked firmly behind me. I could not turn away. There was nowhere I could run.

The burn ward had me.

1

A Life of Privilege

NO TWO PEOPLE RESPOND TO THE SAME THING THE same way. But the one thing I did share with everyone else was the five-minute obligation.

I was born in 1992, at a time when the Hindu-Muslim riots were at their peak. Two thousand people lost their lives in the name of religion that year. I was born to a Brahmin Hindu father and an Iranian Parsi mother. When my mother was fourteen years old, her parents had moved to a little fishing town on the outskirts of Maharashtra called Dhanu.

That is how I landed in Dhanu. At that time, it was a sleepy town that made most of its income from fishing and chikoo farming, while a balloon factory nearby provided employment to a majority of the locals. My mother describes my birth as a nightmare. She says that I couldn't help but make trouble from the word go; she called me 'trouble' before I even drew my first breath. At about noon on the 13th of October, two weeks before I was actually due, my mother declared national emergency because she couldn't feel me kicking. People told her to enjoy the peace and quiet because I was quite the hyperactive foetus and had caused her many a sleepless night. She nevertheless insisted that she be taken to the hospital. The hospital, a tiny run-down building, performed their tests with their meagre medical equipment and revealed that my heart beat was slowing down. My mother panicked.

The doctors decided to perform an emergency C-section because the umbilical cord, which had wound itself around my neck, had decreased the circulation to my brain, and I was in imminent danger of accidental strangulation. My mom honestly believes that those few moments of oxygen deprivation is to be blamed for the way I eventually turned out. Slightly off-kilter. Eccentric. This is not a proven theory however. Besides, I don't think I'm all that eccentric. When my mother wouldn't stop hyperventilating, she received a resounding slap from her *masi*. That instantly restored normalcy to her readings and the doctors could safely and quickly perform the procedure. I was born at 2 p.m. My father, grandparents and aunt were informed of my premature arrival and they jumped onto the next flight to see how I had turned out. My father walked into the room and said I looked like a rat. It was certainly not a love-at-first-sight moment for him. I don't blame him. I did look pretty gruesome for the first couple of weeks.

My parents had met at a rock concert in Delhi and had instantly fallen in love. Amnesty International was hosting a charity concert that brought together some amazing international talent. He was my mother's first boyfriend and within the next fortnight or so, they were betrothed. 'Now that I think back on it, the fact that they met at a "charity" concert may be the only tie that linked me to my future career. The arrangement did come with its fair share of drama. She was a Parsi and a woman to boot. Although Parsi men are allowed to marry outside the community, Parsi women have to toe the line and marry within the community. If not, they are ostracised from their communities and never allowed into the fire temple ever again (wow, what a punishment!). The speed with which my parents were married is the same speed with which their marriage deteriorated. My mother had to move to Delhi and adjust into a very orthodox Brahmin joint family. My extremely religious grandparents hold the concept of God very close to their hearts. I was the apple of everyone's eyes, although they (i.e., my paternal and maternal relatives) never quite saw eye to eye in all other matters. I was their first grandchild.

I was raised and schooled in Delhi and had a relatively normal childhood. I spent my summers in Dhanu swinging from chikoo trees, eating *bhel puri* by the beach, and torturing hapless mud crabs because they fascinated me. I was extremely pampered by my family and got almost everything I had my heart set on. My father was a young pilot at the time. He had skipped college and gone straight to flying school to become a pilot. He aspired to follow in the footsteps of my grandfather, who in his time had been the director of operations for Air India as well as a highly-respected senior pilot. My parents were brave enough to get divorced when I was seven years old. At the time, divorces were unheard of and frowned upon. Whenever I told someone my parents were divorced, they would apologise like someone had died and I never quite understood it. I looked up to my parents because they chose happiness above everything else.

The divorce didn't go down very well with my grandparents who already thought the concept of a love marriage was insane. They were heartbroken and concerned about the repercussions from society upon the family. They had every reason to think this way though—divorces at the time weren't the norm but an exception in India. After the divorce, everything changed. My mother moved out and was doing her best to find employment and my father was always flying. For a woman who had never held a job in her life, was married straight out of college and now had to suddenly fend for herself in a city where she had no family, my mother was making it all look far too easy. Watching her conquer her struggles as a single mother is where my initial fascination with the strength of a woman began. I was raised by my grandparents for quite some time in the meanwhile. I fondly remember my childhood school mornings. I was woken up by my grandmother who would bathe me while I was still half-asleep. She would make it a point to chant the Hanuman

Chalisa every morning as she poured warm water over my head. It is no surprise that I managed to memorise the very long spiritual chant and can remember it even today. We worshipped a godman called Sai Baba; I was the talk of my entire extended family when the *baba* actually placed his hand on my head and blessed me. At the time, I knew nothing about devotion and was more intrigued by the way he could make expensive objects appear out of thin air by waving his hands. I never actually yearned for any of these gifts; a Barbie would have sufficed.

Over the weekends, I would visit my mother and on the nights when my dad was home, he would cook with me. We dabbled in everything from mozzarella sticks to pasta and never ate any of it. Every now and then, my father would take me on extravagant holiday jaunts and elaborate shopping sprees to buy me 'pink' clothes. He would be delighted when a saleswoman mistook him for my brother. After the divorce, my father sank into some sort of an early mid-life crisis that I didn't really understand. It is safe to say that he had his fair share of relationships. This one time he brought home a foreigner and, even though I thought it was pretty cool, when she sat in on bhajans with my grandmother, we were all nonplussed. I'm not saying that someone who is not from our culture cannot participate in it; I'm just saying it was a funny picture. Considering that a love marriage with an Indian was such a big deal in the first place, this unconventional *saas-bahu* duo really did blow my mind. She was a nice lady though; it's a pity that she broke my father's heart and abandoned him. Perhaps it was for the best. At that point, he desperately needed the distraction, but I did feel bad for him. Oh well!

I struggled in school because academics were never my strength. My parents were frequently called in to discuss my antics and they hated parent-teacher meets. In the 7th grade it was decided that I would be put into an international school that followed the International Baccalaureate Curriculum. This curriculum allowed students to not only explore academics, but also focus on creative fields like designing and art.

The fancy school was set in the foothills of the Arawali mountain range and I was to live there during the week and come home on weekends. I didn't mind though; this school was like heaven on earth. It was everything a boarding school technically shouldn't be. We had laundry service and a salad bar at lunch and dinner. All the students belonged to affluent families that could afford the lavish arrangements. Everybody's parents were somebody here, and we all had something in common—we were children who were dearly loved but could not be looked after because of our specific and special needs. The school ensured that all the children found subjects they were passionate about and even though most of us failed our academics, we had more resources to concentrate on things we were actually good at unlike the other generic schools.

Despite being a rebel at heart, I was finally doing well in school in some subjects. I enjoyed getting into trouble and throwing tantrums—not something I am proud of—but not something I would hide either. I went through phases of progression and then, depending on my mood that day, would destroy all my progress in one fell swoop. One particular weekend, when I was in the 9th grade, I returned home to find my father missing. I learnt from my grandparents that he had moved out and was living with a woman whom I had called *masi* for the longest time. Monica had been a friend of the family since before I was born. I had grown up with her, her two daughters and her husband (whom she had divorced as well by this point). At first it came as a shock and I was livid. How could he have left without telling me or warning me? Was this the only question that raged in my mind? I felt betrayed. Angry. And rather confused. I lashed out. I vented my spleen at everyone and everything including my teachers, my schoolwork, my friends and even myself. I began to self-harm in a pattern of attention-seeking behaviour. After my father left the house and moved in with his now serious girlfriend and fiancé, I made it my party pad, had friends over at all hours and we did things which were neither age nor health appropriate.

I never had a shortage of anything. The worse my tantrum, the more easily would my guilt-ridden father give in to my demands. He often tried to persuade me to meet the woman who was soon to be my step-mother, but I adamantly refused. I however met up with my soon-to-be step-sisters because I had grown up with them and held no grudge towards them. They were in the same boat as I was. By the time I reached 11th grade, I had worked all the mischief out of my system; I moved into the apartment in Gurgaon where my father lived with my step-mother and my two step-sisters. Things got much better at this point. I channelled the same ideology I had adopted when my parents got divorced about wanting to see my parents happy, and it was all good after that. I was happy that two people who had failed at love previously, had managed to get a second shot at it. In my family we don't really use the word 'step' anymore because it feels like we had always been destined to be a family.

And then I applied for college.

2

Fashioned Differently

I NEVER REALLY WANTED TO STUDY FASHION. ART, ON the other hand, was something that piqued my interest. I was all set to pursue my dream, when my father decided it was a waste of hard-earned money to learn to dab with a paintbrush for three whole years. In any case, he said, it wasn't a lucrative line and wouldn't help me in the future. I was, naturally, crestfallen. He nudged me towards a fashion course instead, a subject that had absolutely no relevance to my life, at least not the way I wanted to live it. Regardless, by some miracle, the Leeds College of Art saw some potential in me. Leeds became the stage from which the next three years of my life would play out.

Don't get me wrong: I loved dressing up and getting all dolled up as much as the next person, but at that juncture it seemed rather pointless to spend time studying what people liked to wear, or what absurdly extravagant amount some rich soul had splurged on an average shopping spree. More than anything, it felt inanely superficial to be judging someone on the basis of their physical appearance.

I didn't want to study what was on the outside. It would not challenge my grey cells and it made me wonder why people considered it a tough subject; I mean seriously, how hard could it be to analyse something so materialistic and shallow? Just how difficult could it be to keep up with the fake 'artists' who thought their 'creation' was the ultimate pièce de résistance?

The subject on which I was about to base my entire career didn't breathe passion—it rang hollow. It was a BA (Hons) degree in being judgemental, because what it basically entailed was casting a jaundiced eye on a person's exterior—and never mind if an individual's style reflected their unique personality and was both pleasing and affordable on some level. It could be passed off as 'fashion' in any case, because someone somewhere thought it was exclusive and absurd enough to stand out.

Because these garments lacked purpose and were obviously not fit to be actually worn, they were put under the category 'avant garde'. This was borderline costume-ish but apparently, for those who truly understood it, it was 'art'. Now that is something I would like to show Da Vinci in person. I have a feeling he would either laugh at our ignorance or would prefer to be buried with the Mona Lisa, before anything and everything was passed off as 'art'.

With the rapidly changing seasons and styles of haute couture over the years, people seemed to be running out of trends. How could you not? There are only so many things one could actually brainwash the economy into wearing.

Garments came into fashion and then went out; a couple of years later, the same things came in and exited again, and the cycle continued. When previous trends returned, they would be considered 'new' because a certain aspect (e.g., colour) would be subtly altered and suddenly it would be all the rage once again. It was a flea market; the designers were sales people selling anything that they could get away with. As soon as you have a few people wearing your things, everybody wants them. This only goes to prove that no one wants to be unique; everyone wants to be 'in fashion'. It is shallow because it differentiates people on the basis of what they wear and how they look in what they wear—where's the equality in that? Someone once said that art is what you can get away with. Considering that it's a fairly accurate description of the fashion industry, I guess it truly is art. Just not as personal and it actually matters if you walk out in public with something you can't get away with. I was so full of my very original theory.

As with everything in my life, I was about to be proved wrong.

I completely misjudged what I was studying and this realisation didn't dawn on me until my third year of college. I literally faked my way through the first two years of college, displaying no sense of personal style whatsoever and my lack of interest was as evident as global warming. I related fashion to clothes, trends, being superficial, money and every other thing that didn't interest me. When I got to my third year, I found that I could use everything I had learnt in my first and second years and do whatever I wanted with it. This filled me with a new-found sense of freedom and I couldn't wait to take full advantage of it. I didn't realise it then, but I was exactly where I was destined to be, studying exactly what I was supposed to be studying and my father was about to find out that he didn't waste his money by putting me through fashion college.

But everything changed when I went home for my Christmas break that year. In the months to come, I was about to find out how my fashion degree would empower me to address issues in my country that didn't affect me as much as they ought to have.

3

The Infamous December of 2012

I ALWAYS HAD THE ADVANTAGE OF IGNORANCE. Walking into every chapter of my life, I was slow to understand what it all actually meant. What always came to my rescue was my spontaneity, which however made me jump into all the wrong situations, and if I had been wise enough to have realised that, I probably wouldn't have had some of the experiences that I am proud of today.

December 2012.

If you are a young individual living in India, you tend to have this habit—it is called 'going for a drive'. This is nothing more than what it suggests. If you are bored, or even if you are not, you could simply hop into a car and go for a drive with one of your friends and just 'catch up'. Late night drives on the other hand are a more common practice as the youth in this country somehow love the thrill of feeling invincible. Or the idea of it.

I loved it too. Either it was the thrill of invincibility in a dangerous country, or us being oblivious to the danger, or maybe we were in denial. Until December 2012.

I was an adrenaline junkie loving my lifestyle, living in ignorant bliss, carelessly brushing off my parents' pleas to avoid these late-night jaunts with my equally foolhardy friends. 'What can possibly happen to me?' I would retaliate and out I was in the dead of the night enjoying my freedom. I never once thought of what it was like to be a girl in New Delhi. Reality didn't ever hit home enough.

17 December 2012.

I had decided to meet up with a friend and casually strolled out of my house with my mom shrieking in the background about 'some rape case' that had just taken place. *When one lived in India, news of rape, dreadful as it is, is an everyday occurrence and life didn't exactly screech to a halt each time; therefore, my mother's urgent entreaty didn't deter me in the least.*

It didn't in the least bit make walking out of the door a scary proposition, because if you live in India, you get to hear about rape cases every day. While she continued to make a fair bit of noise, I retorted with the supreme nonchalance of the typical teenaged brat, 'Mom, chill out! We live in India, for god's sake. This happens every day. Get over it!'

Now when I think back, the fact that I was okay with this happening every day, just speaks volumes about the kind person I used to be. Either way, mom went on with her hysterical rant and I walked out as I always did. My friends were also subjected to the same behaviour from their parents, so we decided to just channel our invincibility and walk out, for the night was young and New Delhi was our playground.

I hopped into my friend's car and we drove around for a while. Eventually we decided to stop in a residential colony and chatted. We were just settling into a hysterical anecdote when a neighbourhood security guard/watchman tapped on the car window. This again was common practice, so we just rolled down our windows and started yelling at him for interrupting our conversation. This man though, seemed like he had seen a ghost as he asked us in a hushed whisper, 'Haven't you heard about the rape case? It's not safe to be out at this time. Delhi is not a safe place.' We laughed at him and told him that nothing was going to happen to us and to leave us alone, as was our standard response to this routine interruption. We carried on with our banter and at about 2 a.m., decided to call it a night.

18 December 2012.

I woke up to my mother hollering about yet another rape case. By now, fed up of hearing about 'this' rape case, I decided to turn on the television and watch the breaking news myself. At first, I didn't quite understand what was happening; I just saw chaos and from what I understood, there was this girl, 23 years old, who had been gang raped and was fighting for her life in the hospital. I felt bad, but then again this happened every day and I just didn't understand why the media seemed so agitated over it. After all, incidents like this happened every other day, and they never bothered to raise such a hue and cry. I turned off the television with a sigh, blaming the media for my indifference. 'What was so special about this girl? Seriously, the media should get their priorities straight. How lame!' I went on with my day,

The Nirbhaya gang rape slowly dawned upon my generation, a generation which always seemed late to react to every piece of important information. People everywhere were earnestly discussing the rape and to pretend as if I knew what was going on, I moaned about how my mother forced me to watch the news; sadly, that was my only contribution and point of view on the case at the time. It's even sadder that I thought that remark was worth being called a contribution.

19 December 2012.

By now this rape case had gathered an insane amount of attention. It was everywhere and I felt 'left out' because I didn't know any details about it. I decided to pay heed to my mother's nagging and knuckled down to watch the news. Sometimes I wish I hadn't but that wouldn't have made any difference at all because a storm was gathering and no one and nothing could stop it. When I switched on the television's news that day, I had no idea that it was going to change me. A girl had been gang-raped. She and her friend had been picked up from a mall in Saket, a mall that I frequented; this fact brought it close to home and gave Saket a morbid feel. It was just getting worse by the moment as details from this rape case came to light—my stomach started churning and I felt like I was going to throw up. This was no ordinary rape case; this horrific incident was about to start a revolution in India and I didn't even know it. This girl was gang raped and tortured, she was bitten and beaten, she was stripped naked and thrown onto the street. The accused used rusted iron rods to scoop out her insides. They threw her intestines on the street and threw her out of a moving bus like she was an object. I just didn't get it. It just didn't make any sense! WHAT? This was so beyond my level of understanding. I was gobsmacked; this didn't happen to me per se but I could very easily have been that girl. This didn't happen to me but as I sat there and saw new information surface, why did I feel like that girl was me? Why did I feel her pain so deeply? Why did I cry myself to sleep that night? This wasn't me—sorry but I was shallow and I possibly shouldn't have been so affected but I was and it was the oddest feeling I have ever had.

The rest of December 2012.

I had officially become a hermit now. I was so paranoid about going out that I just sat at home and shut out the world. Even if I did venture out, Delhi was no longer my playground. Delhi had become a place where nightmares stalked the streets. I didn't want to be out on the streets where I had previously felt invincible. I wasn't invulnerable anymore and that I understood loud and clear. That's it, my illusion had ended. I knew exactly where I was and I knew for a fact that where I was, was no place for a girl to feel invincible. I don't think this rape case hit my friends as hard as it hit me though. They all seemed affected and no one could stop talking about it, but they still went out and lived their lives thinking and firmly believing that this couldn't happen to them. They had this relationship with their mythical immunity that allowed them to go on like nothing had happened. On the other hand, I grew more cautious and began to follow the news religiously. I even apologised to the media in my mind and thanked them for giving the case the attention that it deserved and not burying it, and for showing ignorant and indifferent girls like me that this could very easily have been me. I know exactly when my friends started getting bothered by this though: it was when the New Delhi club curfew began.

New Delhi was not a fun place to be in anymore. The capital's nightlife had dwindled to nothingness. Delhi had every reason to be boastful before but now it was paying for the crimes that it had not sheltered an innocent girl from. It had all vanished before our eyes. The shiny disco lights, commercial tunes blaring, the sparklers that would come out with cheers every time someone popped a bottle of champagne, it was all gone. Every club would shut early and that's if they didn't shut down altogether due to lack of business. Police check posts were at every corner to cast a damper on the few brave spirits who dared to still venture out. Everything just died—the partying, the going out, the drunk driving, EVERYTHING! Delhi was at a standstill—I saw protests on the television daily but not once did I have the courage to go join any of them. My parents advised me to stay indoors most of the time and since I was to leave to return to college in the UK soon anyway, I was more than content to remain in the comfort of my own home. I was usually reluctant to return to college after a great holiday in Delhi, but this time was different. I couldn't wait. I couldn't wait to walk on the street not being tormented by the demons in my head that had recently turned me into a god-fearing person.

Nirbhaya was the name they gave her; her true identity was not revealed at the time. Some called her 'braveheart' and people from all over the world prayed for her speedy recovery. At one point, the government had to fly her out to Singapore as her condition deteriorated and you could almost hear the chants for her wellbeing on everyone's lips. Nirbhaya died thirteen days after her attack but she did not die in vain. All of India, from politicians to students, celebrities to paupers, to every person you could name, including inmates in jail, were united in grief and anger. When the finger-pointing began, the general public laid the blame squarely on the government for failing to protect India's daughter, Nirbhaya.

Nirbhaya had now become the 'Daughter of India'. Not only did she deserve every part of that title, but everyone truly believed it for the first time. Also, for the first time, I saw people from every walk of life unite to address one issue, and not have opposing points of view on it. I had to leave India for college at this juncture, but that didn't stop me from devoting a part of my day surfing the internet to follow the developments on this case. My friends and teachers in college would ask me about it, and it wasn't about just Nirbhaya anymore, it was about India. They would ask me if it was safe to live there. If I got harassed in public places. It was hard to explain to them that, before this, I was a part of the callous two per cent of the population that neither noticed nor cared what the people in my country had to deal with on a daily basis—who lived or died or was raped. The world was now pointing fingers at the Indian judicial system. Fast-track courts were introduced, so was stricter policing. The protests continued and India finally woke up.

It changed everything.

4

Leeding the Way

THE MINI REVOLUTION IN INDIA HAD BEGUN TO subside now. Although the club culture of New Delhi never really resuscitated, the youth found new diversions to keep themselves busy. I was a little less scared now. One would have assumed that the death sentence awarded to the accused in Nirbhaya's case would have considerably reduced the number of rape cases, but sadly, it only made things worse. I don't know if Nirbhaya made it easier for other girls to come out and report crimes that were being inflicted on them or if the media chose to highlight every rape case now; nonetheless, rape was everywhere. Most claimed that 'India was raped' and we could now pride ourselves on being the 'rape capital of the world'. I mean, what else could it be? If we weren't, these incidents wouldn't be happening so much even now. I don't know if I had gotten used to hearing about rape again and again or if I had given up on the idea that it would ever stop.

My third year of college was in full swing. I was so overburdened with work that I barely had time to breathe. My goal was to merely scrape through somehow. My head of department at the Leeds College of Art was a lady called Suzy Mason. Suzy stood tall at 5 feet 1 inch and had short wavy hair; she always wore interesting clothes and epitomised creative genius. Suzy had recently joined LCA and all I knew about her was that she didn't like me but to be honest, Suzy didn't seem to like a lot of people. She was stern and never withheld her 'constructive criticism'. It is funny how the majority of my class could be scared stiff of her (myself included, of course) when she looked so harmless. It is not like Suzy ever yelled at anyone, but she had an acid tongue and that, I think, was the scary part. I was dreading 3rd year with her because I was afraid that she would write me off as the unenthusiastic student that I actually was. There was just no faking it with her. I had no clue, of course, that Suzy was about to become the catalyst that would initiate my journey into a world that was way beyond my comfort zone—all the way from Leeds in the United Kingdom to New Delhi in India. My first module was fairly simple—I could do whatever I wanted. I was finding it hard to correlate fashion to women's rights and that's when Suzy encouraged me to look at other designers who had managed to achieve this. She succeeded in guiding me, and I was truly inspired. I started looking into the work of Katherine Hamnett, a designer who created T-shirts with relevant political quotes on them (long before it was considered 'cool'). Her work was simple and hard-hitting. I soon realised that fashion could be equated with one's ideals. This was the first time in three years that I had had such an epiphany, so for me, it was like walking into a whole new world. I was excited. I remember Suzy telling me this one time, 'Fashion is not about designing clothes and silhouettes. It's a type of communication; it's the first way we all express ourselves. Fashion is so much more.' Perhaps if Suzy had walked into my life two years earlier I wouldn't have 'just passed' and would have actually created something more meaningful—but better late than never, I suppose.

My first module ended with me handing in a fashion film shot in India portraying the suppressed Indian woman. I designed a plastic underwear. Yes, a see through, transparent plastic underwear. The concept was clear (pun intended); okay maybe the concept wasn't that clear, but the underwear was. I had one of my best friends, Mehr, wear the clear underwear that had little slots in it, slots which held fabric pieces that had generic descriptions of what an Indian woman was expected to be, 'obedient, fair, soft-spoken, etc.' printed on them. The two-minute fashion film literally comprised of Mehr slowly pulling each piece of fabric out of her plastic underwear until she was left bare and broken down. It is safe to say that my mind hadn't progressed to a great level of intellect at this point, so the film was creepy and slightly eerie because I chose to have Indian chants play in the background to give it more character. Somehow it all came together and it was a hit with Suzy! I was beyond thrilled.

She actually liked my work! Now that I had the interest of my harshest critic, I knew I could do anything.

After the first module came the dreaded Final Major Project, which we called 'FMP' to make it sound slightly less intimidating. FMP had a nice harmless ring to it. Nonetheless, if you were a fashion student in the UK, you would know for a fact that FMP was your ticket to the world as a designer. I hadn't a clue about how I was going to step it up a notch after my last module because that was the hardest I had ever worked. And to be honest, I was flat out of ideas. It had taken me so long to find the first one that I knew I was doomed the second time around. For our FMP we had to submit a total of six products and since my course didn't directly entail fashion designing itself, these products could range from conducting events to creating websites to styling. The flexibility we got probably contributed to what was to come next.

Everyone was well into their final major projects and I was desperately seeking inspiration. I was jealous of all my fellow course mates and cattily decided it must be extremely exhausting for them to stay 'inspired' all the time because this state of mind entails being swayed by everything. This is not a proven theory, just my interpretation of inventive and innovative genius. My concepts are different now, but those were what they were back then. For example: There is only one happiness in the world, to love and to be loved—Rumi.

See I don't agree with this. I believe there is much more to happiness. When I was inspired I found beauty and ideas in everything; everywhere I looked there was a new approach just waiting to captivate my mind, just waiting to talk to me. Sadly, nothing was talking to me at the moment and trying to be inspired within limited time didn't help expedite the process. It only made it harder. I couldn't force inspiration to bestow its beatitude on me, it just wasn't happening. People around me didn't understand that; they thought it was just another one of my ploys to delay knuckling down to work. While others around me plugged away, I found myself surfing the internet in search of ideas. How could I relate women's empowerment with fashion yet again? God knows it was no cakewalk the first time around.

The thing is, it is hard enough to capture the attention of self-centred kids of my age and even harder to get us to focus on someone else's point of view for more than five minutes, and then too out of some kind of compulsion or obligation than courtesy, also known as 'the five-minute obligation' according to me.

While still trying to figure out what my FMP ought to be about, I stumbled upon a photo of an acid-attack victim in India. I had watched the documentary about Katie Piper, a survivor of acid violence in the UK, a couple of years ago. As usual, the five-minute obligation got the better of me. I had been so captivated by rape that I never really gave much thought to any other form of violence.

Now that rape was dealt with in my last module, I found myself drawn into a new form of violence—acid attacks.

The first image I ever saw of an Indian acid survivor was of a 15-year-old girl called Tuba. Tuba's face barely looked human anymore. It was shocking how a 'simple' act of hurling lining acid on someone's face could alter their appearance so drastically. I just couldn't wrap my head around it! It made me want to look deeper. 'Why did this happen? How could this happen? What did this even mean?' When Tuba raised her hand to her face in some pictures, the human element of her intact hand created a jarring comparison in my mind. I don't know what it was honestly, it didn't make sense. When I saw the mutilated face above her unharmed body, it was the strangest feeling. I was intrigued. I spent that night looking at various acid-attack cases and my research was inconclusive because it looked like the same victims had different names on different websites. 'Who were these girls really?' Their images drifting across the world wide web with different names, different stories, yet with one common feature—they had all been robbed of their faces. My pink bedroom was plastered with these faces, projected on my walls with the help of my imagination. The more I gazed at these faces, the more they morphed, the more I looked at every little detail, every bump, every imperfection, the more beautiful they appeared to me. Their scars were like puzzle pieces, each one of them had a story to tell and like an obsessive puzzle solver, I had to know more.

I was deep in thought when my British flatmate and best friend knocked to ask if I wanted something to eat. I jumped at her offer and seized the opportunity to forget and redeem my five-minute obligation card. Fran had this amazing ability to talk about the most random of things and take my mind off everything else around me, but her superpowers were proving to be a little weak today and I couldn't shake Tuba's face out of my mind. I tried to appeal to the self-centred 21-year-old in me, but she failed to rise to the bait as well. When all else failed, I tried to distract myself with my fresh break-up which would normally throw me fifteen feet deep into a shaft of hardcore depression and self-pity, but nothing invaded my thoughts as much as Tuba's face. My obsession that had lasted only an hour by then, was starting to scare me now.

I am squeamish by nature, a perfect girlie stereotype, ergo the obsession with the colour pink; priding myself on being daddy's little princess; the affluent Indian who could actually afford an education abroad; an Indian girl without a pronounced Indian accent; the girl with the chihuahua. I could tick every box on the cliché checklist. I enjoyed my weekend clubbing in London with my flamboyant friends, not caring about how I spent my father's money, of which he didn't have very much. Just because he could afford this education for me after years of saving up, didn't mean he could actually afford my pretentious lifestyle. However, he silently bore my shenanigans and I exploited the situation more than I should have. I was insensitive, entitled and ignorant, but I was just like everyone around me. It was normal. Tuba's face didn't make me squeamish, it just intrigued me; what was the story there? I was defying my own stereotype. The five-minute obligation had officially been broken and after dinner that night, I went on to watch a documentary on acid-attack survivors in Pakistan called 'Saving Face'.

5

The Photoshop Effect

COLLEGE IN THE UNITED KINGDOM HAD ALWAYS BEEN my dream. Growing up in India, one ends up creating these fantasies about college life that hardly ever live up to one's expectations. Most of these are star-struck delusions straight out of the movies—the wild parties, coming home at odd hours—basically throwing away three years of your life using education as an excuse to escape orthodox India. When I finally went to college, even though it didn't live up to any of my dreams, it was no less a fairy tale. I revelled in the freedom; the whole experience was so special that I always knew that leaving it all behind would be a wrench.

After being preoccupied with 'Saving Face' for two whole days now, I found myself sitting in Suzy's office, which was situated across the hall from the third-year studios. You would normally only see third-year students having one-on-one talks with Suzy in this office, discussing the future of their FMP. It was quite easily the scariest place to be. One required to book a slot in advance to even get in. The silence of that room normally got to me; it was where my dreams came to die because my dreams, as supremely superficial as they were, were the sort that Suzy invariably saw through and immediately relegated to the rejection pile, where they truly belonged.

That brisk and rainy day, I found myself face-to-face with my biggest critic. Well into the semester and I had nothing to show for it, except share with her my innermost thoughts that were hijacked by acid attacks. This had absolutely nothing to do with fashion; I had no ideas, nothing! I sat patiently while Suzy typed out an email on her Mac desktop which made it even more excruciating. After she was done, she looked at me and gave me a smile and asked me what I had done so far. I took out images of some of the victims that I had printed out and slid them over, saying, 'I don't know what I'm going to do with this, but it has been playing on my mind and I feel like I want to do something about it.'

Any other professor would have replied, 'What do you mean you want to "do something about this"? Is that all you've got, the idea that you *might* want to "do something about this"?' and that's exactly what I waited for her to say. But she surprised me. She carefully examined the pictures and then said, 'Then what are you doing here?' I was shocked. I didn't even know how to react because I really didn't know what she meant. 'If you want to do something about what's happening in India, you can't do it all the way from here, now can you? Stop wasting your time in the studio, the victims are not here.' Within seconds it was decided that I was going to spend the last semester of college back home in India.

At that moment I was pretty sure that I had bitten off more than I could possibly chew. The shallow me caught up with me—and all I could think about was being away from this amazing life and getting my hands dirty. I thought about this being my last semester and how everyone would have so much more fun than me. And that when I grow up, I would have to tell my children how I spent my last semester in the United Kingdom ... in India. It was going to be a sad story. I am glad Suzy urged me to board the next flight back home, but it wasn't easy. I telephoned my father and told him that I was returning home and he simply laughed in disbelief. I don't really blame him; I didn't even have a plan. All I knew was that my college was equipping me with a video camera and a whole lot of space to explore the world of acid attacks. I knew I could talk my dad into anything. I wasn't sure if I wanted to talk him into this, but I did. There would be no looking back from here on.

Someone once said, 'Beauty is only skin deep.' Then someone else said, 'Beauty is in the eye of the beholder.' Both were dead right.

As I packed to leave for India, I was already in touch with my first survivor. Her name was Radha. I was corresponding with the hosts of a campaign that worked towards eliminating acid attacks in India and had planned a makeover project for one of the survivors. I wanted to film it as part of my FMP. Yes, I know what you are thinking. You are probably wondering why I was doing something so utterly superficial as a makeover when I had a chance to do a live interview with an acid-attack survivor. I have no qualms in admitting the idea was actually a rip-off and not my own at all. I had seen a video on survivors of cancer and each one of them was given a complete makeover. When they finally got to see themselves again, it was magical. At that moment everyone involved in that video was immortal. Did you know that when you create something so beautiful, you can live by it for the rest of your life? I had a tattoo on my right hand which I had gotten on my 18th birthday. It symbolised strength and immortality. My understanding of it was overcoming the obstacles in my life and being immortal through those achievements. I believe in moments that make one immortal, moments through which one could vicariously live the rest of one's life, no questions asked. A true example of that one immortalising video was what I aimed to capture.

I had started talking to Radha on the telephone even before I reached India just to familiarise myself with the person she was. The first time that I spoke to her, I was stunned! She was just like you and me. I don't know what I expected. It's not as though an acid-attack survivor would sound any different in a telephonic conversation. But it was just astonishing. I think it was the realisation that I could be a mere phone call away from a face that was starting to wholly captivate my every waking and sleeping thought. Radha's character beamed right through that long-distance call; I didn't have to talk to her very long to nickname her 'Bunny'.

Another survivor I spoke to was called Sanjana. Sanjana was the coordinator who was in touch with most survivors in India, almost creating a network of sorts, which was news to me. I didn't think the survivors had a network or knew each other or even helped each other. But what did I know, anyway? I knew what Radha looked like because her pictures were all over the internet, but Sanjana was nowhere to be found. I stumbled across this one shot of Sanjana however, her entire face was covered except for her eyes, of which one eye was missing. The skin around the eyes looked old and puckered, and furthermore the image was slightly pixelated so I couldn't really tell. Since I had managed to find only one snap, I wasn't even sure whether the girl in the photograph was Sanjana.

It was exciting. I found myself thinking of Martin, Maison Margiela, the 'missing face' of the fashion scene and he seemed to have the same intriguing effect on me as the survivors. Margiela was a designer no one had ever seen. He never came to his own fashion shows and always worked behind the scenes. There was something beyond mysterious about him. His high-end shops were always situated in quaint locations with minimalistic signage that made him even more enigmatic. Sanjana was now my Margiela.

By the time I actually boarded my flight to India, I had established a relationship with Radha on the phone and I couldn't wait to meet her. I was so ecstatic that the nine-hour flight couldn't wipe the smile off my face. I knew I wasn't going to regret my decision. I knew I wouldn't miss the partying, the freedom, my friends, anything. My journey was just starting and everything that came before this seemed pretty vacuous. For once the turbulence as we circled over New Delhi didn't bother me at all. Normally, the grating of the wheels emerging from their housing before landing would shatter my peace of mind, leaving me stricken with pangs of anxiety. But this time, everything was different. The wheels came out and by now I was so excited that even if this aeroplane didn't land, I would have probably parachuted myself down anyway! Why was I so excited? I wasn't going clubbing or meeting my boyfriend (which I didn't have). I didn't get a wink of sleep all night, but I didn't even need coffee to keep me up! I landed and rushed straight home. My mother (like all mothers) welcomed me with an affectionate hug and a gentle kiss on my forehead; she knew I hated it, but she did it anyway! I shrugged off the wet kiss and dashed into the shower.

I got ready, heaping on the make-up. I simply had to look perfect. Mom sat on the bed watching my every move. She asked me: 'Why are you putting on so much make-up? You're going to meet someone who doesn't have the same luxury.'

I didn't even stop to think about what she had just said. This was how my face always looked. This was my look; not wearing make-up didn't even cross my mind because the make-up was my face. I was never without it. I wanted to look my best when Radha saw me. For some odd reason I felt I had to impress her. Despite everything she had been through, I had no sympathy for her, but I admired her strength and courage, something that I didn't possess. Somehow, I thought if I looked my best, it would make up for my other deficiencies. After my long make-up session, I was out the door.

Radha's house was a good two hours away from mine and I decided to catnap on the way.

I was woken up by my chauffeur in the middle of a desolate village. This was rare for a city like Delhi where there was never a shortage of humans. The village didn't seem like it was in the city at all and it was as if time had stopped here. I felt I had wandered into an episode of *Malgudi Days*. How authentic, I thought to myself. Armed with my camera, I telephoned Radha as I got out of my car. Luckily, we were right outside her house. She walked out to greet me, her face covered. We were still walking towards each other and drawing closer when suddenly she flung herself forward, enveloping me in a warm bear hug. I hugged her right back. She grabbed my hand and we walked to her house with a bounce in our steps. In her single-bedroom house, her aunt offered me a cup of tea. Unlike most people, I wasn't a big fan of tea, but in that moment, I would have drunk anything. I just felt privileged to even be invited into someone's home. As I sipped my tea, Radha removed the *scarf* that covered her face and I was overwhelmed by my own reaction. Because I just didn't have one. A face that had captured my every waking and sleeping thought would have warranted some sort of reaction, wouldn't it? Maybe one heart flutter or even teensy-weensy tear. Was I a monster? Radha started narrating her story to me. She was attacked by her stepmother in the middle of the night while she was asleep. The time when she should have been dreaming, soon became her worst nightmare. Radha had been sojourning in her native village at the time. She was aware that her stepmother resented her. She called the village a 'sleepy town' because when she was attacked at 10 p.m. and ran out for help, the streets were deserted. She banged on doors and roused her neighbours before she received any sort of assistance. She was eventually taken to the hospital, five whole hours after the vicious attack. I had recently found out that if the acid is brought into contact with water within the first three seconds after the attack, there will be minimal scarring. It takes more than three seconds for the brain to even process what has happened. You can't even feel the pain until a couple of minutes later because of the shock. The quicker the acid is neutralised with water, the greater the chance of saving primary organs. At this point, small town hospitals aren't even aware of how to neutralise an acid attack, so one could not expect mere mortals to know what to do. You are given a three-second window by science to literally save face. Radha went untreated for five hours.

After our lovely meeting, I bid Radha and her family goodbye. As I sat in my car, trying to marshal my thoughts in a bid to understand why I didn't feel anything specific when I saw Radha's face, it hit me. I had been talking to Radha for a while now and she had managed to become a friend. When you truly like someone as a human being, their appearance doesn't really matter. Would you stop loving your best friend any less if she became fat? Does a blind person who likes you for who you are recoil when he or she touches your hand and it isn't as smooth as he or she imagined it would be? Do they judge you by that touch? I chose to apply the same logic here. Because if I didn't, I would worry that I had no feelings. It made sense to me now, everything that I had grown up around, the conditioning, the superficiality, it was starting to melt. I think I was finally starting to understand the meaning of relationships and what it meant to not judge a book by its cover. The journey home was full of introspection; I was trying to make sense of this world, the suffering and the love, and the conclusion I came to was that I was witnessing the strength of the human spirit in all its glory and boy, did I feel honoured to be able to do so.

6

The Burns Ward

SOMEWHERE ALONG THE SHOOTING OF THE documentary, someone had reached out to me to ask if I could help raise funds for a survivor. I had been told that this survivor, Rekha, was in dire need of help. Rekha was from Bangalore and had been attacked by her husband because he thought she was cheating on him. This man happened to also be a rickshaw driver and obviously some sort of closet mechanic because he didn't attack her with just any acid, he had drained battery acid and had doused her with that while she was asleep. The week after I was informed about her case, I went to Bangalore to check on Rekha. I was supposed to also meet another victim who was responsible for showing me around. It was only after I actually met her that I realised that my guide, Haseena, had been blinded in the attack.

Haseena was an inspiration. Even though she had lost her vision, she had put herself through blind school, knew how to use her cell phone effortlessly, was a pro on her computer and her list of achievements just went on. Within the first few hours of our meeting, Haseena was turning into my role model.

The hospital was an hour away from Haseena's house, but our journey was filled with conversation, debates and laughter. As soon as we reached the hospital, Haseena felt it was her moral responsibility to warn me of the horrors that lay ahead. And for good reason. She knew that what I was about to witness would haunt and torment me forever. She knew, with the clairvoyance of someone who had been to hell and back, that by the time I emerged from the ward, I would realise that I had walked into a relentless nightmare.

Victoria Hospital, a government-run hospital, is affiliated with the Bangalore Medical College, and has now been renamed Bangalore Medical College and Research Institute. It is the largest hospital in the IT City, set up in 1901 by Shri Krishnaraja Wodeyar, the erstwhile Maharaja of Mysore. Despite its royal heritage, it is pretty much like any other government hospital in India—with standards that would not be acceptable anywhere else in the world.

Once through the door, it took me a while to accept the fact that I was actually there. No amount of forewarning would have prepared me for what I saw, heard and felt.

Firstly, thanks to my ignorance, I had no idea that a ward meant there were more than two patients per room. I also somehow managed to miss out the part that a ward did not have any rooms at all. This one in fact had sixty beds, to be specific, and endless floor space where the less fortunate patients lay. The doctor who was showing us around had a pleasant face and a warm personality that seemed to put me at ease. She warned me that no photography was allowed inside the ward and I soon knew why.

I could not stick to my original plan of breezing through the ward, eyes shut, until I reached my victim Rekha's bed. Since Haseena was with me, I had to guide her. So my eyes had to be wide open and my steps, painfully slow. And my brain was to register the blood-curdling sights, sounds and odour.

Every step I took, seemed to take me deeper and deeper into a horror film scene. Or worse. I was shocked beyond words. Almost numb. It seemed a never-ending walk to Rekha's bed at the end of the ward. I walked past women with disfigured faces. In some cases, the face did not even exist. All these women had one thing in common—they were all victims of that one-second of anger that had corroded off their existence. The value of human life or the lack of it, was painfully visible.

As we neared Rekha's bed, I saw this girl sitting upright on her bed. And she just sat there. She was burnt from head to toe and she just sat there. It would have given me more comfort if she had cried or yelled or screamed because that is what normal, sane human beings would do. But then it hit me—she was not sane and why would she be? She turned towards our approaching footsteps and kept waving at us in a slow, almost agonizing pace.

As I got closer to Rekha, I braced myself. She had no face. Her eyes were bandaged and since Haseena was visually impaired, neither of them could see the horror on my ashen face. Haseena felt me trembling and grabbed my hand to tell me silently that it was going to be all right. I felt weak, foolish. I had always thought I was a strong one. But this moment, this day told me that I knew nothing.

Rekha was too weak to talk, and we thought it would be best that she be allowed to rest. We were about to leave when the doctor asked us if we would like to meet another victim—an acid-attack case that had just come in. Judging by Rekha's condition, I didn't even want to imagine what this 'fresh' case would be like. But this ward left nothing to imagination. As much as I didn't have the courage to, I obviously had to talk to her. After all, what kind of a social worker walks away from a victim? My kind. I was perhaps better off sitting in Delhi, reading up about acid-attack victims. Raising funds. Theoretically I knew everything there was to know about them. I knew that when someone threw acid on you, your face started to melt and fume and practically burn off right on the spot. Having met Rekha, I knew what it was like to live that nightmare. I signalled to the doctor that I was ready to see this new victim and we again took slow, painful steps to the other end of the ward. I closed my eyes for a brief second before looking at her face and when I did, I was stunned. Her face was fine. It was normal. I could tell she was in pain and I could see where the acid had hit her because it was about three shades darker than her skin tone, but she was fine. Features intact and everything! I was almost thrilled.

Maybe this was reversible, I was suddenly optimistic. She was going to be just fine and she was the lucky one. My euphoria was short-lived. The doctor told me to take a good look at her and when I started off about how lucky she was, the doctor burst out laughing. A bit insensitive, I thought to myself. But she went on to ask if I actually knew how acid worked. I had a sinking feeling that I was about to be proved wrong about everything I knew, yet again.

The doctor began to explain that acid was a substance that once thrown on someone, cannot be retracted. The first few days in the life of an acid-attack victim were probably the only good ones she would ever have. The darker shades of skin that I could see, would start to disintegrate in a couple of days. The area would rip, bleed and melt. These darker patches would destroy all semblance to a human face and eat away this innocent girl's identity.

As I listened to these words and looked at her face, I was overwhelmed with the urge to shake her, show her a mirror and tell her that this was as normal as her face was ever going to be. I wanted her to see her face, admire it and then say goodbye to it because she had no idea what lay in store for her.

I now knew why victims had so much hope, because they too believed that acid worked in the way I thought it did. The painful part was the illusion of hope that these darker patches gave to the victims. Her face was like looking into the past, looking at something that no longer existed, something that would cease to be in the days to come. I did not see this one coming. I did not think that an intact face could be so much more horrifying that the absence of one.

At that moment, everything I thought I knew, believed and had faith in, was destroyed.

Welcome to the burn ward they said. Your life will never be the same and trust me, they were right.

7

Getting Serious About It

ON OUR DRIVE BACK TO HASEENA'S HOUSE, WE SAT IN silence. And all of us—Haseena, her mother and I—knew why. Haseena had undergone forty-six facial surgeries and the family had visited the hospital enough number of times to understand the mess I was in. They seemed to respect my space and let me be. I was grateful.

At the house, as soon as we had settled down, Haseena's lovely, cheerful sister, radiant with the glow of pregnancy, handed me a glass of water. Sensing the reason for our silence, she enquired, 'How bad was it?' with a smile on her face. She was contagious, and I chuckled wryly as I broke my vow of silence, 'Well—'

At this point Haseena and her mom decided to join in with the good humour, all of us united in the unspoken belief that if we choose to smile in the face of our fears, our fears don't stand a chance. The pall that had settled on us lifted and we started chatting about the ward in a manner that didn't send shivers down my spine.

I think I adopted my dark sense of humour from the survivors who had realised that the only way they could survive the ordeal was by making light of the situation. I told them how horrified and helpless I felt because I had never seen so much misery and despair, or witnessed an atmosphere more void of positivity, and that I didn't think I could ever be the same. Most importantly, I asked them how to get over it.

I was sitting right next to Haseena, who placed the palm of her hand on my leg and softly said I would never get over this because I was destined to help.

The survivors had no faith in a system that had only let them down, but Haseena had faith in a 21-year-old, when no one else did. I found it inspiring and humbling. She almost had me convinced that I was to be a saviour of sorts but, just as I began getting comfortable with the idea, I came crashing back to reality. I couldn't do anything because I had never been capable of doing anything at all. However, I played along with Haseena and agreed at that moment because I didn't want to dampen her spirits. I didn't quite know how to break it to her that I wasn't going to be this movement's catalyst.

Only recently, acid attacks had managed to get their own laws, but every aspect of those laws lacked legalities related to implementation.

Government hospitals were not equipped to handle such intensive burns, there was no information about how to deal with it on first aid, there were no statistics on the number of victims. Survivors were dying because their government and judicial system were letting them down. The attackers were still at large. In the midst of all this, a fashion student wasn't going to be their messiah.

I hugged Haseena and her family goodbye, thanked them for their hospitality and left for the airport. My journey was consumed with flashbacks of the ward. It felt surreal because I still could not believe that such a place existed. I wanted a sense of adventure and answers for my documentary but it felt like I was leaving with more questions than explanations.

It was a hopeless situation with a grand total of two organisations working on the ground, one of them being a campaigning organisation. I realised that there was a dire need to address what was happening. How could all these deaths and crimes go unnoticed and unpunished? The nebulous idea that I could and should make a difference was taking shape. I reached the airport two hours prior to my flight and decided to get a foot massage. Mid foot massage, it dawned on me that sitting in a darkened room with your dark thoughts probably wasn't the best idea.

When I returned from Bangalore, I got straight to work and by 'work' I mean I had no idea what I was doing. The end game would be to create some sort of social impact and help the survivors but unfortunately, I didn't even know the 'S' of survivor, let alone the 'N' of the three-letter acronym 'NGO'. I just knew I had to start somewhere so I sat with my laptop to try and figure out how to set up an NGO. About two minutes into my research I realised I would require a chartered accountant to register the organisation and then I would have to break the news to my parents and my tutors in the UK who still believed that I was filming a documentary. I started with the easier of the two and telephoned my stepmother to enquire about a CA. I was in luck—she instantly messaged me the number without evincing even an ounce of curiosity. On the not-so-lucky side, I had a Skype session with Suzy in two hours.

I planned to make the most of the internet speed that a developing country has to offer and decided that if the conversation didn't go smoothly, I would simply disconnect and blame it on the connection. Three rings into the call and Suzy answered. We spent the first two minutes exchanging mandatory pleasantries and then she came to the point—how was the film going? Funnily enough, I would always call it a documentary and she would reply saying 'filllmmm' in a very British accent. This time however, I used the word 'film' to play along. I paused, pondered over the difference between film and documentary and then said: 'About the documentary, Suzy ... I'm not making it anymore. I am going to start an organisation.'

I swear if Suzy wasn't Skyping, she would have burst out laughing. But both of us showed the good sense to not react. Suzy proceeded to gently, but sternly, ask me what that actually meant. Even though I thought I had made myself quite clear, I realised she wanted me to elaborate on my plan of action. Naturally, I didn't have the answers to any of those questions, so I did what I did best—I faked it. I started quoting sections of NGO registrations and had she googled even one of them, she would have known that I was lying. But she seemed pretty convinced by my zero knowledge on the IPC, but did it matter that the Indian Penal Code had nothing to do with this? I quoted it anyway. It was only the next day that I found out from my very informative CA, Rahul, that we would be registered under the Societies Act.

To my surprise Suzy seemed pretty all right about me starting up an organisation, even though it had nothing to do with fashion. One critic down, it was time to confront the parents. What I would soon realise is that no one actually took me seriously. They had absolutely no problem with me setting up an organisation that helped individuals who were disfigured and disabled. I mentioned it in passing and the only concern that my father seemed to have was that I would not be returning to the UK anytime soon. He mumbled something about what a waste of money my undergraduate degree had been because I chose to leave the very developed UK and come back to the grime and crime of my own country. I don't think he realised that I would soon devote my life to lives marred by violence and that the least of his concerns would be me living in India once again. He had no clue that violence had become an intrinsic part of our lives. This was probably because everybody had implicit faith in my inability to persevere and commit to anything for any length of time.

After a gruelling day with the CA discussing details that zipped past way over my head, I returned home to be greeted by my little chihuahua, Puggie. Puggie was a two-year-old anniversary present from my ex-boyfriend. I had just about plonked into the sofa and opened up Facebook on my iPhone, when the phone rang. It was Haseena. Even though I didn't really want to speak to anyone at that point, Haseena was too pleasant to pass up. Her voice was angelic and she was super understanding. It was a different matter altogether that I had become obsessed with talking to survivors because I felt that they were the only ones who understood me.

One would think that I would feel guilty about unburdening myself to Haseena about the things that upset me. But she had an amazing knack for making me talk. I found myself telling her about my idea about establishing an organisation and the phenomenally bad day I had had that day. My insecurities about being shallow and incapable of understanding a complicated sentence were catching up with me. Before I knew it, I was sobbing to her about the Societies Act and the bylaws and not knowing the difference between a trust and a foundation. It was as if a dam had broken and at that moment I knew I was crying only because I really wanted to help and felt woefully inadequate. Haseena calmed me down and asked if she could speak to my mother. I flounced into my mother's room huffily like a five-year-old, handed her my phone and walked out.

Twenty minutes into the conversation, I walked back into my mother's room to find her sobbing. She tearfully thanked Haseena and said she hoped to meet her some day and handed the phone back to me. Haseena told me that none of it was going to be easy. She said I would even fear for my life sometimes and at others I would have no idea what I was doing. She said that no one would understand how I felt or be able to comprehend the things that I was going to see. But she assured me that she would always be there for me, because she believed in me. Although I felt encouraged, I honestly had no idea what she was talking about. When I look back on that day, I realise that the blind girl had caught a glimpse of my future.

I was up all night researching the NGO sector in India. I started reading about the laws specific to acid attacks and even though it was frustrating that I had to read each thing several times in order to understand it, I did it because someone's life depended on it. If only I had studied this hard for my board exams. I stayed up until 4 a.m. and for the first time in my life, I actually had a small sense of accomplishment when I went to bed. I felt slightly less stupid and I had managed to lay a foundation for myself. I knew I had to start somewhere. And I did.

8

Cut Wide Open

I CAN CREDIT THE EXISTENCE OF MAKE LOVE NOT Scars to my spontaneity. If I wasn't spontaneous, I wouldn't have jumped at the opportunity of visiting that burns ward and if that had never happened, then well ... we would all have a great documentary to watch. But hey, you win some and you lose some. Let's hope I can get back to the video camera one day though; I really do want to complete that documentary. I witness some amazing things every day and some horrible ones too. But that's life.

Being spontaneous is a great thing (sometimes) and at other times, it has you questioning yourself. Just when I thought I had seen enough of everything there was to see, I got invited to witness a surgery.

Like a fool, I accepted. While it is great to know everything about your field of work, maybe learning about surgeries through theory and not watching the practicals would have been a smarter idea. But I was on a roll. I was naive enough to think that I could handle just about anything. I did not realise that I would only start becoming desensitised two years into my journey and not four months in.

The doctor who invited me to watch a surgery being performed, had obtained permission by stating that I would be recording footage for research and that I was a doctor myself.

I was cool with the first part of this elaborate lie, but I knew the second one would be harder to fake.

The surgery was scheduled for a Saturday and I reached the hospital right on time, excited, nervous and obviously not realising what I had gotten myself into this time. My enthusiasm about getting a more hands-on perspective about the medical aspect of my work as a social worker had gotten the better of me, I guess.

The gravity of the situation really hit me when I walked into the ICU. I saw several semi-conscious and unconscious souls recovering in post-operative care. I think it is safe to say, I was flabbergasted. I seriously contemplated faking an illness and scarpering, but it was too late. I was cordially escorted into the nurses' changing room and given a clean pair of scrubs. The small changing room had a full-length mirror on one of the walls. As I stared at my strange reflection, I wanted to smack myself in the face for what I was putting myself through. I struggled with disentangling the strings of the trousers. Perhaps it was a sign ... or maybe my hands were just too clammy to undo the knot! After a couple of minutes of grappling, I got into my combat gear, a far-from-intimidating powder-blue and mint-green hair cap. I neatly tucked my hair into the beret and donned the face mask and slipped on the shoe covers over the hospital slippers. The thought of other people's feet having been in them was beginning to prey on my mind. I think it was also my mind playing tricks to keep me distracted with trivialities and stubbornly refusing to dwell on the doom that loomed large.

Suited up, all that I needed to do now was take a selfie.

After all, I was walking in to witness a surgery, so what was the harm in a picture of myself to remember what I looked like at that moment in my life? I emerged from the changing room, handed my cell phone to the nurse and I couldn't even vent about how nervous I was because she thought I was a doctor.

I recall those moments as they slowed down to an eternity.

I am taking slow steps, deep breaths as I pass the beds with patients. They seem to be drifting in and out of consciousness—that's scaring me. I'm glad however to be wearing this mask, and you can only see my eyes. Thankfully, I don't believe that the eyes are the window to the soul. The first door opens, I'm relieved that it is just an ante-room to wash your hands and not actually the OT. But wait! This room doesn't have a door and I can see an unconscious survivor on the operation table as I scrub my hands.

Anxiety consumes me or maybe it is grief, I don't know, I can't put my finger on this feeling, let alone put it in words. I take a long time to wash my hands when the nurse that's watching my every move tells me to hurry up. I dry my hands quickly, shore up my spine and walk with determination towards the table; the doctor who invited me greets me. He introduces me as 'Dr Sharma' and the pressure to remain sane and conscious is on full throttle.

Let's call the survivor Laila. Laila was out cold on the table. I had no idea that operating tables didn't have cushioning, they were just steel. That's a bit harsh, I think to myself—as though she wouldn't be sore enough after surgery, she might even wake up with an inexplicable back ache. Laila has a tube down her throat; a team of five doctors hover around the theatre working on various parts of Laila's body. I start from her feet that were facing me and see a team of two doctors operating on her abdomen. Her shirt is pulled up halfway and there is a large incision under her belly button towards the lower right. Given that it was a big gash, it is a wonder that it is not bleeding.

The main doctor starts explaining the procedure; I am barely cognisant and certainly not prepared when he suddenly raises the incision flap to reveal her insides.

I jump in shock, unable to keep it together. The other doctors watch as the lead doctor holds up a device that looks like a balloon attached to a pipe. The entire apparatus is transparent. He explains how the balloon would be inserted into her stomach and sewn shut leaving the pipe hanging outside her body. Over the next few weeks-months, they plan to inject saline water through this pipe to gradually inflate the balloon inside her body thereby expanding her skin. This would then allow the doctors to have more skin to work with for her next surgery. Laila is skinny and I wonder how this could actually work. But then I was no doctor.

The doctors test the device by filling it with saline and I am guided towards her head. On my way, I pass a table that seems to have thin strips of what looks like chicken breast on it. I wonder if it is fake skin or flesh. I don't have to wonder long because soon enough, from my peripheral vision, I see a doctor neatly removing grafts of flesh from Laila's forearm.

Again, a shocker there—barely any blood! They scrape off one layer with what I think is a scalpel, but I could very well be wrong. He then stretches it and neatly places it on the table. I want to vomit. I try to ignore what's happening and continue my journey to the top. I reach the top and I suddenly want to go right back to the bottom, back through the hand-washing room, backtrack to the ICU, through the changing room, take back my phone, undo the selfie and the changing of clothes, rewind my steps out of the hospital, back into the car and press play, skipping this episode of my visit to the hospital altogether.

There's a large, large chunk of the top of her head missing. The chunk is not deep but quite wide; blood covers a bright white surface and Laila seems like she's in the deepest slumber of her life.

I am finding it hard to cope now, I actually do not understand what is happening. I don't think I even *want* to understand, but I don't really have a choice. I am desperate to take a break, but I don't want to seem ungrateful for the experience. The doctor that works on Laila's head is handed a piece of flesh from the 'chicken breast' table; he spreads it on the open patch on her head and starts trimming it into shape. Yes, he actually starts to cut the pieces of her flesh, which have been sliced off of her arm to fit the humongous opening on her head. He spreads it out flat, and as soon as he is satisfied that he has the perfect size, he starts to sew on the edges to the parts of unharmed flesh. I notice that the flesh he's sewing on is very thin compared to the normal skin on her head and I wonder if she's going to be left with a deformed scalp. As the doctor starts sewing, he glances at me and asks, 'Is this how you do your stitches, doctor?'

HUH?! Should I totally wing it and make up a story about how I do my stitches? I'm afraid I didn't even know there was more than one type of stitch. I nod stiffly, 'Yes, I do them exactly like that', and then give the game away by asking him what the underlying white surface is. His eyes widen askance as if I have asked him how many days there are in a week. I think he has caught on now and knows I'm not a doctor, because he bluntly replies, 'That ... *Dr* Sharma ... is the skull.' I'm mortified for a bunch of reasons right now.

1. H-how-ow could I not know that was the skull or did I maybe know that on some level but was in shock and disbelief?
2. Duh, that was the skull, what else could it be? I think I presumed it was protected by a thicker layer of skin maybe?
3. My cover is blown or maybe not, maybe he just thinks I'm a really bad doctor.

Okay, let us be realistic, my cover is blown. Damn!

The head doctor catches on and quickly changes the topic in order to save me some embarrassment. He asks me if I'd like to have some soup. I don't even know if he's being serious to be honest, I mean this had to be a joke, right? I could barely keep down my own vomit, did he want me to wash it down with some soup? Did he forget I wasn't actually a doctor and this was not normal for me? Did he forget that I had never seen a body being cut up before? Did he forget that under such circumstances it would be very odd for me to be hungry and the image of raw chicken breast was still stuck in my head? I politely decline the soup.

I decide to take a break and sit on the side—this is when I am told that the surgery will take four more hours. Let's keep in mind this is after I walked into the surgery four hours after it had actually started because I was told to be there for the last two hours of the procedure only. After about two hours, I find myself moving around more comfortably. I am actually enjoying watching the procedure and am fascinated by the possibilities. After my cover was blown, the skull doctor explained to me how the new graft of skin, even though it was fairly thin in comparison, would eventually grow to the density of the rest of the skin on her head. It is mind-blowing to think a thin piece of human tissue was capable of that! I start to make friends with the pieces of flesh lying on the table as well, examining them, observing their stringy fibrous consistency. I hold the balloon like device and feel the texture of the plastic that it was made of and scrutinise the other medical equipment. By the end of three hours, I am all right. I am comfortable with the situation that I find myself in and I feel content knowing that the wise owls were always right—they say that the only way to eliminate one's fears is to face them.

I am definitely not done struggling to cope with the situation, but I am moving past my initial shock and trying to embrace the beauty of medicine. I always had a high regard for doctors but now I have a new respect for them. To go through such procedures on a daily basis and yet be so normal, for the sake of saving lives, is easier said than done.

But I have spoken too soon.

As we neared the four-hour mark and Laila was all stitched up and being bandaged, a large sponge-like object is cut to shape and wedged into the space between the fresh skin graft on her scalp and the gauze. The sponge is secured with bandages very tightly to ensure that the graft doesn't fall off while it is healing. Her stomach is neatly sewn shut with the tiny pipe hanging out and bandaged. Her arm is bandaged and the last thing left to do was to make a small incision near her left eye to release the tension that the hardened skin was causing. I have seen enough by this point not to be intimidated by a small cut, so I actually stand in and watch closely while the skull doctor makes the incision. He inserts his scalpel into the point where the incision should start and carefully slices downwards.

At that very second my left eye starts twitching and my heart starts palpitating. I think it is probably because it was only in this moment that I was actually looking at Laila's face directly and could feel her pain. I touched my face to make sure I wasn't hallucinating and to my surprise, I am not! I am in pain. It is real, physical pain. I feel overwhelmed by this strange capacity I have discovered in myself to empathise so deeply with the victim that I can actually sense her suffering. I hare off into the hand-wash area, rip off the face mask and peer at my face in the mirror. I am rclieved to discover that I have a stye and not some inexplicable connection with Laila. I wipe off the sweat beading on my forehead and when I stroll back into the operation theatre, I find that they have started to revive Laila. I know the anaesthesia has started wearing off when Laila starts groaning; the doctors are talking to her softly, assuring her that she is all right even though she isn't conscious yet. They tell her that she is still in the operation theatre and that she should stay calm while they retract the pipe from her throat. I cannot even begin to imagine her agony at this juncture. Two doctors hold her body straight and another one holds her head while the skull doctor tries to manoeuvre the pipe. At this point Laila is gradually coming to and suddenly her body starts twitching as though she is having a seizure. Everyone still seems pretty calm and I don't see any special machines produced, so I presume it is all normal. But it is proving to be one of the most terrifying things that I have ever seen. Perhaps the surgeons were prepared for this and that was why they had held down her body beforehand. They continue talking to her all the while, asking her to calm down while they struggle to remove the pipe even as her body is convulsing. When they finally take the pipe out, Laila is still writhing in pain and making noises I wish I can forget.

I have never heard such shrieks, like her throat is dry but she still needs to convey the intensity of pain she is feeling. It is heart-breaking and I have had just about enough.

I don't think it is appropriate to say goodbye, so I walk out of the operation theatre without telling anyone and return to the changing room. This walk is different however; I am unfazed by the other semi-conscious bodies and I breeze past them with no expression on my face or in my heart. I am numb but surprisingly, completely composed. I change my clothes, collect my phone and walk out of the hospital.

I sit quietly in my car and wonder how I can even begin to describe what I saw to my family and friends. How could I get them to relate? How could I show them that people suffer in the worst possible ways while we worry about such inconsequential problems? How was I ever going to explain all of this to them?

Eventually I try my best to explain but decide to skip the gore. I realise that they are better off in their ignorance. On the outside I will always be who I used to be, but on the inside, I am changed. And the struggle from this point onwards will be to figure out how to see these things and still retain my sanity. I have chosen a calling and what I have been through took place in a very controlled environment no matter how traumatic it seemed to me at the time. I have to be prepared for a time when I would witness such misery and have to be the one to console others. Reality had hit, a make-it-or-break-it battle had begun to rage within me daring me not to lose myself.

9

Make Love Not Scars

I HAD STOOD IN ON A SURGERY, HEARD AMPLE survivor stories, ran a fundraising campaign to help a survivor with medical procedures, studied the laws, met with lawyers and researched procedures that would not be available in India for the next decade at least. I had conducted one photo shoot with the survivors to try and help with communication and I put up a Facebook page to help me spread this information and raise awareness about my campaigns. My bylaws were ready and I had managed to bring eight people on board in order to register the NGO. It didn't matter that most of this panel happened to be my family members. I was enthused; Make Love Not Scars was finally ready to be registered.

My Facebook page was 5,000 followers strong, which at the time seemed like a milestone I would never be able to top. My new identity was the 'acid-attack girl'. Friends and acquaintances I had not spoken to in years wrote to say how very proud they were of me. I think some of them were just intrigued, maybe even amused, but most of them were surprised. A few of these brave individuals would even state that they were amazed at my 'transformation'. I wasn't sure whether to take this as a compliment, but I was enjoying all the attention I was getting regardless. People would enquire about volunteering and I had managed to set up a strong volunteer network by now. This came in handy when I decided to organise a launch event for the NGO.

The launch was scheduled for 4 April 2014 and if there is one thing that I pride myself on, it is how to throw a party! When I started planning the event however, it dawned on me that this would prove to be a very different 'party' to the ones I was used to. My guest list was drastically different and trying to involve other social activists to attend was no walk in the park. Getting a sponsor for the venue, catering and coming up with a suitable theme were other hurdles that one had to overcome but if I could study an entire cause from scratch, I knew I could do anything. I had a lot of help and found that everyone was always ready to provide in the name of a good cause. It is something that I would find myself capitalizing a lot on. Forgive the bad pun, but acid attack was a burning issue at the time. Until that point, there had never been any help for acid-attack survivors. It was new and there was a certain curiosity about it. Acid-attack survivors had only recently started coming out openly in the media, willing to share their stories in order to spread more awareness. The same way that I was initially intrigued by their stories and the lack of information on them, others were too. This was the season to be helpful and that's what everyone did. They helped in ways for which I would never be able to thank them enough.

Finally, it was 4 April 2014, and I found myself in a nervous frenzy, running around, trying to put the finishing touches for my event. The survivors and guests were walking in and the stage was set. The launch was at an upscale mall in Delhi hosted generously by a beauty parlour. I wanted to give the survivors a day to feel beautiful, so I decided to give them all makeovers. The concept of a 'makeover' could swing both ways. People could finally realise that the acid-attack survivors were just like us; sometimes they wanted to let their hair down and get all dolled up, and that could be a point of appreciation. Or, they could criticise me for changing their appearance. The way I saw it, if I could put on my own make-up and no one found it offensive as it was a part of my identity, then this really shouldn't be a problem. They are one of us after all, right? The survivors would get beautified while guests were free to circulate around and spend their time interacting with them. I managed to rope in a fancy Anita Dongre outfit for Sapna as she got her make-up done by the best beautician in town. The event would culminate with the unveiling of all the beautiful makeovers, both the artists and their models, and a short speech by me about what Make Love Not Scars was to be. The evening seemed to be going swimmingly and in all the excitement, I forgot to put on make-up. My friends and family were astonished and so was I! My father was the first to gently point it out, and then my mother, and then every other person that walked in; they just weren't used to seeing me without my 'face'. This got me thinking about the first time I met an acid-attack survivor; she refused to uncover her face in public not because she was uncomfortable with it but because she was uncomfortable with the way people around her may feel. I would always urge my first survivor to walk around freely and not be ashamed of what someone else had done to her. It was ironic that all the while I camouflaged myself behind a thick layer of make-up. I don't think I did this intentionally, I was just used to caking on the make-up and that became my face.

So, when I always hid behind maquillage, I probably shouldn't have been preaching about makeovers, but I did. I always thought that my job would be done on the day that my girls felt confident enough to roam around freely. I felt that that would be the day when society would welcome them with open arms and the survivors would no longer have anything to worry about. Half the problem with an acid attack, aside from the obvious pain and suffering that everyone is aware of, is how hard people around the survivor make it for them. Furthermore, acid attacks at this point are a form of gender-based violence and we live in a male-dominated society that is intolerant of a woman making her mark.

Our women are frequently judged purely on the basis of their appearance. When a woman exercises her right to say 'no', she is brutally disfigured because 'if he can't have her, no one else can'. This notion in itself says so much more about the society we live in and less about the attacker. The fact that the attacker believes that if he disfigures a woman, she will no longer be accepted, is a massive failure on our part. We collectively endorse his belief that a woman's worth is measured by her outward appearance—and not by her intellect or talent. I had started to believe that acid attacks were a form of violence that we had brought upon ourselves. If we had ensured that the worth of a woman was so much more than her outward appearance, then perhaps the attacker would have realised that his efforts to destroy a face would be in vain.

Today however, these women are held in contempt and suspected of having committed a terrible transgression to have been so severely punished. Is it even possible to do anything bad enough to deserve this? The whole concept, the problem and our understanding of it, is dated. The survivors not only found it hard to get treatment after an attack, it was nigh impossible to fight the government for their rights to their compensation. Technically, the measly government compensation of rupees three lakhs was to be given to them no later than one month after the attack so that they could use these funds for their recovery. This rarely happened and years on, survivors would beg courts to release to them what was rightfully theirs. If this wasn't bad enough, they were denied jobs due to their disfigurement, which led to more financial instability and caused families to split up leaving survivors abandoned and alone, reinforcing the idea that this was their fault somehow. Now imagine going through all of this and knowing that the man that did this to you is still a free soul, roaming the streets of Sunday bazaars, eating *gol gappa*s while you rot in a confined space and blame yourself for all the problems that have plagued you and your family since the attack. It was clear that the situation was dire and while I was adamant on changing all of it, I knew by then that baby steps were the only way to go. If we had to fight this long battle, the true fight would have to come from the survivors themselves and in order to do that, they had to be empowered.

Mid thought, I was nudged by a volunteer who said it was time for me to address the gathering. I started by thanking everyone for coming to the event while my friends and family cheered me on. We had some journalists present as well, who were there to get their scoops about the acid-attack survivors. I started talking about what Make Love Not Scars aimed to achieve and what it was going to be, which basically summed up fighting all the factors I was cogitating earlier. I brought up the part about how society should start being more accepting and ended with, 'There is no reason for the survivors to hide behind their veils, their face is not their shame. No face ever is.' Or so I thought. And then it came out like verbal diarrhoea, 'and so I have decided to not hide behind my veil any longer. I pledge that I will go make-up-free for the next 365 days.' Everyone cheered while my family stood in shock; my friends were confused; I obviously hadn't realised that frivolous statements no longer had any place in my life. I was accountable now. And seriously. That's where it began, Make Love Not Scars, my 365 days without make-up and obtaining a deeper understanding of the society we lived in, not solely from a survivor's perspective, this time from mine. The rest of the event flowed beautifully. Vidya Tikari, a renowned make-up artist, spun her magic on Sapna who wore a generously donated Anita Dongre outfit. The other survivors all got makeovers while the guests floated from one survivor to the other asking them about their stories. It was an evening to remember and everyone who was there was inspired to help this 'new' cause. More than everyone else though, the survivors left that evening feeling more comfortable and accepted and that is something that will always be incomparable to any other great feeling I have known.

The next one year became an uphill personal battle. People no longer looked at me the way they used to. You know that moment at a club, when you are all dressed up with your make-up on, and you are the cynosure of all eyes. Well, that stopped for me. My eyes lacked the sparkle brought on by the skilful application of highlighter and mascara. My former intentionally flushed cheeks were now pale and my lips no longer seemed as luscious. An acquaintance once walked up to me at a club and was caught off guard. 'Woah, hey Ria, didn't recognise you there!' and I don't know whether he was tipsy or if he just lacked an understanding of social awareness, but he proceeded to say: 'Been doing a lot of cocaine recently, eh? It's starting to show on your face.' At that moment I was so embarrassed that I didn't bother giving him an earful and merely defended my appearance by stating that it was for a good cause. He immediately admired my nobility. It was funny because in that moment I only felt like a great big loser. However, a few days later something happened that would leave me feeling like less of a loser and would enforce why I championed this particular cause.

So I walked into a survivor's house and she looks at me and asks if I'm feeling all right. I knew why she asked me that question, or I at least thought I did, but I just wanted to hear her reason anyway. She told me I didn't look well and that I looked pale (something I already knew) and there it was, the cherry atop the cake that I would relish to mitigate my gloom. More worn down than I already was, I quickly pulled myself together because that's what social workers do, right? They are always hopeful and chirpy and whatnot. So that's what I did; in spite of how I looked and felt about it, I knew someone needed me more. I explained to her that I decided to quit make-up for a year and that now we could walk around outside without our veils on. To my surprise, she burst out laughing and asked me why on earth I would take up such a pledge. I wanted to tell her who I did it for and to express to her how ungrateful she was sounding because I had just literally renounced my soul for her, in girly terms.

But I did not do that. I just smiled in a saintly way, like giving up make-up was no big deal and told her that it really wasn't that big a sacrifice. In retrospect, that was one of the biggest whoppers that I had ever told. After hours of persuasion I finally managed to get my survivor to take a walk with me without her veil to a nearby market. I think she sensed by now that this whole no make-up thing was really affecting me, so she agreed. We were both extremely nervous and held hands as we ventured forth like a couple of heroes. We were bare-faced, just being ourselves and if that wasn't enough for anyone, then so be it. Okay, it really wasn't that dramatic, but come on! This girl hadn't stepped out without her face covered for four whole years! It was a special day. So, we walked, people stared and I could tell that this made her deeply uncomfortable; in an instance my insecurities faded and I felt as shallow as an empty swimming pool. I put on a brave face and squeezed her hand and told her she had nothing to worry about. She looked at me and quipped: 'I told you, you shouldn't have stopped wearing make-up; now everyone's staring at us!'

That was it, that was all I needed to put an end to every insecurity I had—her ability to be so amusing, so optimistic and so real, made me realise there was so much more to life than one's appearance. If she could walk around with half a face, who was to complain about a full face?

It was abundantly clear that there was no place in society for girls who didn't abide by its rules. Girls have to look pretty, go that extra mile and spend hours painting their faces, waxing their entire bodies and then be funny, charming, sexy, intellectual and cute all at the same time. It was exhausting and if only my natural dark circles could speak, they'd tell people to take a hint and go. I eventually got comfortable in my own skin. I spent one college graduation, one birthday and multiple media appearances without a vestige of make-up but slipped up every once in a while and painted my face in the comfort of my own bathroom. When society was cruel to girls like me, I couldn't begin to imagine its attitude to my survivors. It put into perspective what I was fighting for and I officially felt alienated from my own sect of society; nevertheless, it was the best thing to have happened. I slowly realised that I wasn't the one saving the survivors.

They were saving me.

10

Monica's Path to Parsons

MONICA SINGH WAS INTRODUCED TO ME THROUGH another NGO. I remember waiting to meet her in my living room and somehow everything I had heard about her wasn't about to do her justice. She walked in wearing a tight, red, full-sleeved polo-neck with a pair of really cute, floral-printed, pastel pants. I thought Monica was Monica's friend. She walked into my grandparents' house and my first thought was: 'Woah, she's a hottie!' Even though those were the first thoughts to cross my mind, my pessimistic brain then went on to question whether she actually needed help. I didn't really know why I was meeting Monica honestly, but at this point I was eager to know. Monica walked in and took my breath away, she was even more stunning in close up. She had had a lot of plastic surgery but what could you expect? She was a survivor after all, but she was still stunning. She was tall, her body made for a ramp model and as I learnt later, she used to be one. A model whose face was stolen from her.

Her story starts in her foundation year of college. Her father was posted in Lucknow and Monica studied in New Delhi. During her holidays, Monica would visit her parents and stay with them for a couple of months. It was that time of the year again when the students flocked away from the capital to spend time with their families. Like any other student, Monica followed suit, even though she now wishes she hadn't.

The unfortunate incident occurred when Monica was back home. 'I was driving when I got a telephone call. My friend got me to roll down my window, claiming to have seen me at a traffic light. I did as he asked and as soon as the glass came down, a guy on a bike drew up alongside my car and threw a cup full of some liquid on me. I was blind-sided. I had no idea what the substance was and assumed it was hot coffee. My first reaction was nothing. I was in shock.' Apparently, the miscreant wanted to marry Monica, but she had big dreams for the future and rejected his proposal. Outraged, the accused plotted to ruin Monica's life and he did, for a couple of years. But what he didn't realise was that this incident only made Monica a more driven person. She underwent over forty-five medical procedures, lost her identity, but never her determination. The next year she went right back to college and eventually graduated with an astonishing 2nd rank degree in all of India!

Monica sat down and for the first time in my life, I was dumbstruck. Should I speak in Hindi? English?

Yeah, that sounds like a superficial query, but sadly, that's the first thing that crossed my mind. Her hair was light brown with blonde, buttery highlights and she could pull off the ideal nerd-cum-sexy look with the large glasses she wore.

'Hey Monica, how are you?' That was all it took for Monica to launch me on a roller-coaster journey. I was about to find myself fighting for something that I always wanted albeit indirectly.

Monica wasted no time; the first thing she said to me was: 'I'm good, it's great to meet you. I just got into Parsons.' That was it. She had me at Parsons. I had always wanted to study at Parsons and I knew for a fact that I wasn't good enough to get in. But this girl was sitting in front of me, had lost her face and almost her life and she studied. She didn't just study, she excelled and that drew me in. This girl got into Parsons and that's where it started and ended. She wasn't a survivor anymore in my eyes, she was an ordinary girl who was special because she got into the college of her dreams. Monica then added, 'I've got in, but I have no money to pay for my education. Don't get me wrong, I'm not begging you for funds, I'm simply asking you to help me achieve my dreams. I'm going to make it anyway and anyhow, but you can help me, I won't deny that. I won't go to the media. No one knows my story, no one has seen my face and I want to keep it that way, not for any other reason but I don't want to use pity as a crutch for my career-path.'

Even though I was beyond inspired by her ideology, I knew I was in trouble. How was I going to get this girl the funds when no one knew who she was? Who would want to fund someone they didn't know anything about? On the horns of a major dilemma, my first instinct was to go for private or corporate funding. Channelling my academic degree, I appealed to the communication student in me. I decided we would make a short film on Monica and use that film to melt the heart of funders. This film was only to be circulated among private funders and that way not a lot of people would know about her. I recruited a brilliant volunteer and we decided to shoot a few days after our first meeting.

I met Monica twice. The first time she showed me her dream, the second time I shot her life and then I left the film in the trusted hands of the other NGO with which I was collaborating and went back to taking care of other survivors. I felt like I had done my bit. I was brought in to make a video that would then be circulated—as I was told—and that was pretty much where my role ended. I wasn't equipped to deal with a $50,000-campaign and even if I wanted to take it on, I really didn't know how. How do you take up such a big project with no experience? I was a 21-year-old, way in over my head with work way above my understanding, trying very hard to get to grips with everything that was being thrown my way at a very fast pace. I was struggling and just about coping, but I knew for a fact that I couldn't manage something like this. Therefore, I didn't even offer to help beyond this.

A few weeks after I had fulfilled my commitment of handing over the video, I assumed that there would have been some progress in her case. I was wrong. When I first met Monica, she had a month and a half to raise the funds she needed. The day she called me, she only had a fortnight left to meet this deadline. Monica was on the telephone and somehow I could sense something was very wrong. She wasn't chirpy or confident. If I had to be blunt, this extremely strong girl was feeling shattered and vulnerable.

When she asked sadly, 'Ria, will I ever go to Parsons?' I was confused and didn't quite know what to say, and what could I say? Her broken voice tugged at my heart and I knew that no matter what, Monica was going to go to Parsons; she deserved to be there.

I replied with confidence, 'Yes, you are going to go. I'm going to try everything I can to ensure that you go.' I didn't know what it was I was going to try just yet, but I knew I had to try something. This girl was so talented, she had stared death in the face without a face, she deserved to study at Parsons. Monica had a total of fourteen days to raise the funds she needed to study at Parsons, $50,000 to be precise, and her fate lay in the hands of a 21-one-year-old, rank amateur.

I sprang into action and the first thing I did was leak her video to the press that night. Yes, that was my genius and insensitive plan. She had told me time and again that she didn't want to share her story with the world but in that moment, I presumed she didn't know what she wanted.

So I did it; I went ahead and did the one thing I was told not to do. The next morning, I woke up to hundreds of positive comments about her video and about a hundred abusive text messages on my phone from Monica. She felt I had betrayed her and let her down badly. I responded by taking screenshots of all the positive comments her video had generated and there was radio silence for a little while. Half an hour later, she called me back and said: 'I'm ready; let's go public.'

I truly believed in two things at this point. First, that if you don't believe in your cause, you should forget about getting somebody else to believe in it. Secondly, the power of social media. I just needed to get the right people to care and I was going to use social media to make this happen. How does one get the right people to care? YOU TWEET EVERYONE. The 'right' people I was referring to was actually just anyone that cared. I tweeted everyone from Obama to Snoop Dogg, Lady Gaga to *Cosmopolitan* Magazine, the *Times of India* to Madhuri Dixit. I even tweeted companies, individuals, and journalists, to the extent that Twitter blocked me out for twenty-four hours because they were convinced I was spamming. Now that, ladies and gentlemen, is dedication. At the end of the day I received a message from a beauty and lifestyle content production house. They offered to help Monica by shooting a fresh video. The next day we were on our way to Mumbai and spent the day shooting, 'Monica's Path to Parsons 2'.

The team at Glamrs worked relentlessly to release the video overnight. It worked—we were viral! Even though everyone in India was watching this video, it wasn't translating into funds and I knew I had to try harder. I emailed the link of the video to various media houses in the hope that they would feature it and after hours and hours of trying, I had CNN Network18 and Dainik Bhaskar lined up to do interviews the next day. This should have been enough, but I wanted to go big, I wanted the *Times of India*. I managed to find their office numbers online and decided I would dedicate my entire day to just calling it as many times as it took until I got a hold of someone to hear me out. I had called them about twenty-five times before they finally gave in and handed me their editor's email address. By this point I was so tired and frustrated that I decided to pen my thoughts down in an email to the editor. The email read as follows:

'Hi sir,

My name is Ria Sharma and I am the founder of a youth-driven organisation called Make Love Not Scars. We work closely with acid-attack survivors and recently we have come across a case that truly deserves your attention.

I met Monica Singh a few months ago and not only did this survivor never come out in the media, but she also graduated with a 2nd rank in India from NIFT. Like that wasn't achievement enough, she astonished everyone when she got into Parsons, New York. I was truly moved by this and because Monica didn't have sufficient funds, I wrote *to literally a million people, hoping someone would help Monica. This company called Glamrs in Mumbai heard my prayers and helped us make a video to aid Monica's Indiegogo campaign which needs to raise $50,000 in order for her to study at Parsons.*

Monica will not only serve as a role model to other acid-attack survivors but to girls all over India if this works out. (or it doesn't)

The only problem is that her campaign only has twenty days left on it, so I took to my computer again to write to everyone I knew. CNN IBN have now decided to film her for their show 'citizen journalist' tomorrow. Daily Bhaskar also published her story on their social media today. All of this exposure will help people know about Monica and the unflagging human spirit that is capable of overcoming anything and everything. You are my last stop and hope. I need everyone to know about Monica.

Below is a link of Monica's video; please have a look at it and if you are not as moved and inspired as I am to send Monica to Parsons then you have every right to not publish this story.

Time is of the essence and I would appreciate it so much if you invested in Monica's dream by helping her spread her story.

Ps- I got your office phone number from a lady called Rakhi who works at TOI *and after calling your office persistently (sorry about that!) I got your e-mail ID from one of your juniors.*

https://www.glamrs.com/inspireme
www.makelovenotscars.org
Warm regards,
Ria Sharma
Founder at MakeLoveNotScars

I decided to call it a night at about 3 a.m. after sending out some more emails. I woke up that Saturday to a call at 6 a.m. It was an unknown number and I answered groggily.

'Hello, is this Ria?'.

I answered, 'Yes.'

'This is the editor of the *Times of India* and I received your email. It moved my wife and me to tears. I think you should wake up, so you can set up an interview for Monica with my journalist. I think we should send her to Parsons.' That morning, I woke up crying. This man had managed to validate all of my efforts in a matter of seconds. I got someone to care. I got the right person to care.

Monica sat down in a coffee shop and narrated her story to the journalist just a couple of hours later. I was moved because just a few days ago this girl didn't even want to share her story, I was taking that in itself as a personal victory. She was going to inspire millions. I always knew that the *Times of India* was a big deal, but I didn't know just how big until I woke up on Sunday at 7 a.m. This waking up early thing was really becoming an unpleasant habit. My mom's shrieks woke me up as she stood by my bedside waving a newspaper in my face.

Monica was on the front page in nationwide print in the Sunday edition of the *Times of India*. Everyone reads the *Sunday Times* and I secretly revelled in the fact that my ex-boyfriend was an ardent reader of the app. He used to read it on the pot every morning and I laughed at the thought of his expression when he saw this. We all have our cheap thrills, right? Exactly thirty minutes after thinking about my ex on a pot, I started receiving calls from multiple news channels wanting to feature Monica's story. Everyone wanted to be amongst the first. I got out my diary and started playing the role of her manager as I scheduled interviews, negotiated with journalists who asked me to put their channel above others and politely declined some interviews that called for weird enactments of the attack. I had never done this before and decided to just follow my gut.

By the end of the first day, our campaign had managed to raise a significant amount of money; it actually felt like we could do this. At the end of the first day, Monica and I sat down, speechless for a few moments as we looked at each other, and then we burst out laughing. We were exhausted and words failed us, but we communicated with merriment at the unbelievable target we had achieved. Neither of us could fathom how this had played out. In that moment we were infinite and immortal; we had just managed to pull off a $50,000 campaign. This was my second campaign ever and it wasn't the worst way to start one's career.

Monica eventually fulfilled her dream of studying at Parsons. We cried happy tears at the airport as we hugged goodbye. She then went on to speak at the United Nations and was valedictorian at her graduation ceremony at Parsons.

11

Anxiety versus Jitender

MY IDEA ABOUT GOOD MENTAL HEALTH WAS THIS—keep oneself happy by doing the things that brought one peace. I actually believed that if you abided by a few golden rules, no mental illness could affect you.

But life does a splendid job of reminding you that no one is invincible. And that your own mind can be a cruel taskmaster.

So there I was, in the first year of my college, in my dorm room getting ready for bed while Grey's Anatomy was playing in the background. I was groggy and was barely listening to the life lessons being imparted by the fictional doctors. After washing my face, I crawled into my cosy bed and surrounded myself with three pillows.

Just as the sandman weighed down my eyelids to consign me to the land of bunnies and cupcakes, I leapt up in sudden panic. It felt like someone had stopped my heart by dropping a rock on it. I frantically Skyped dad and told him that I was having a heart attack. He tried to reason with me and argued that I was too young to have a cardiac arrest. I told him that it was too late. My feet had gone numb and even though I did want to sleep that night, I passed out in a rather inelegant way and keeled over with my head on the keyboard of my laptop. Although my father stubbornly stuck to his heart attack theory, I now had his undivided attention. It's a different story that no one had mine.

I woke up half an hour later to find myself covered in a silver foil blanket with a beautiful man rubbing the soles of my feet while another massaged my palms. Was this paradise?

And then I heard my father's distraught voice in the background and knew that I wasn't in heaven. God wouldn't be that cruel. I turned to the voice to see if he was trying to lure me away from the 'white light' and then realised that dad was still on Skype and I was very much alive. The men rubbing my body were the paramedics who kindly informed me that my anxiety had probably triggered a 'panic attack'. It took me longer than that one night to figure out that you didn't have to be a particularly anxious person to suffer from anxiety and you didn't have to really panic in order to have a panic attack.

As soon as I was diagnosed with anxiety, I started noticing its presence everywhere. Things that had seemed normal in my past now translated into fears that had been dramatised. I started developing mild phobias that ranged from imagining my toes were badly squished within ill-fitting shoes to the fear of flying. I felt like a slave to my own body. On most days, it felt as though the earth was too big, while I was insignificantly small and the fact that it was round, suggested the strong possibility that one could accidentally fall off the globe. That was literally what I wanted to do, jump off the face of this planet. My mind could zoom out of my surroundings at the drop of a hat and before I knew it, I found myself exploring the far realms of outer space and freaking out about the notion of space itself. That's the thing about mental illnesses, they make their presence felt. On the rare occasions that one chooses to ignore it, they persistently knock on the mind's door, until they're acknowledged.

When I started meeting the survivors however, my anxiety was always at bay. My body wouldn't let me be weak in front of someone who needed me to be strong. Correctly speaking, they should have been a trigger but on the contrary, they proved to be my salvation. They became my anti-anxiety pill and I became the addict. Three months into Make Love Not Scars, I seemed to have miraculously healed. I had everything going for me. People were finally taking me a tad more seriously; my survivor network was flourishing and I was actually making some sort of small-scale difference. Visually-abled or partially-sighted survivors were getting to know of a young girl who could actually help them get treatment and blind survivors were hearing about a girl that loved to talk on the phone. I was doing it all.

I had become adept at answering calls from unknown numbers with unbridled excitement because a survivor could be at the other end.

But all that was about to change.

It was 11 a.m. on a lazy Sunday when I received the first call. An unknown number flashed on my screen and I answered with my usual joie de vivre. The caller however, didn't sound bubbly at all. I could tell he wanted to send a strong and harsh message across. He asked me if I liked my face. The fact that I actually took a second to think this through didn't matter to him. He had already assumed I did and I realised that the question was purely rhetorical.

'Do you like your face?' I asked and followed through by requesting the caller's identity.

'If you like your face and want to keep it, you will just go back to the UK or we might have to make an example of you.' I was gobsmacked and before I could respond, he hung up. Along with the phone call came another unwelcome visitor, my anxiety. My body's first and very proactive way of dealing with the situation was to completely break down.

Calls were made to spread a wide dragnet that evening; my father had stepped in and wanted to get to the bottom of this sick joke and his friend, a high-ranking police officer, had immediately sprung into action and traced the number. It was a prepaid one, registered to a dummy address. We realised that this wasn't a sick joke, but a real threat when my father dialled the number and the man who answered told dad that he was a hundred per cent sure that we would never find him. When my father told him that we knew his address, he just laughed. I couldn't believe that this wasn't something from a movie clip. As dramatic as it was playing out to be, we had to give the man credit for being a bona fide death threat artist for sure. We let the situation slide for a few days and thought that it would stop, when I received my second call. I had been prepared to deal with another threat but not for what he was about to say. He told me that I looked very pretty that day and before I could thank him (silly reflex action), he described in detail what I was wearing that day. These weren't threats anymore, I was being stalked and obviously a sitting duck.

That same evening a family meeting was held and the first question I was asked by the judge (my father) was whether I was determined to continue on this chosen career path. Without a second thought about my safety, I replied with a firm YES. It was decided then that precautionary measures were to be taken to keep me safe while I pursued my dreams. That night, however, I started panicking about the future of my face. I looked at my reflection in the mirror and thought of all the cases I had seen and 'keep calm' flew out the window. I incarcerated myself at home for the next two weeks with all the windows and doors locked shut. I would love to have stated here that I was brave and courageous but, let's be honest, that takes time. I found it hard to make the short walk to the kitchen to fix myself my customary midnight snack, which resulted in weight loss as well.

On week three, I met a surprise visitor at the table in the morning. When I and my dark circles walked to the kitchen to grab a cup of coffee, Jitender stood up. I had a mild scare. What was this enormous, six-foot something hulk doing in my house and why did he have a gun? I shut my eyes and counted to ten, but before I could scream he said. 'Hello, madam, *kaise ho*?'

'Madam?'

My mom walked in at the moment and summarily diffused the awkwardness by introducing me to Jitender who had been hired as my bodyguard. I sat down, chuckling, but soon realised they were dead serious. I told Jitender I didn't need a bodyguard because I planned to avoid the meetings for a while and he blandly replied, 'No problem, I'll just come and sit here every day then.' I told him to suit himself and stalked back to my room. Jitender, however, turned out to be one stubborn dude. He was in my living room every day and I would often catch him and mom giggling about what a sissy I was. On the fifth day of Jitender's employment, I finally decided to venture out and attend a meeting. I got dressed and got my things together. I rudely interrupted his game of snake on his Nokia, but the second he saw me dressed up, he jumped up with the enthusiasm of a child going for a treat to the ice-cream parlour. Jitender had previously worked for the government of India and had guarded some very high-profile individuals. Before I walked out of the house, he asked me to put on my sunglasses and cover my face with a scarf. I was just about to tell him that I was a feminist and things didn't quite work like that in my world, but he proceeded to tell me that on the off chance of an actual onslaught, the sunglasses would prevent me from going blind and the scarf would give us the precious few extra seconds to save my identity from being stolen. The scarf was not only a ploy to conceal my identity from a potential assailant but also an additional layer of protection. If attacked, the acid would first come in contact with the fabric which, if I had the presence of mind, I would quickly discard to ensure that the acid didn't come into contact with my skin. It was a long shot and I probably wouldn't have the good sense to react sensibly in such a dire situation, but it made me feel safe in a nostalgic way. The scarf provided the same illusion of security that a comfort blanket would to a child who was scared of monsters under his bed; the sunglasses were like a child's 'magic sunglasses' that would magically endow the wearer with a cloak of invisibility. Whatever Jitender's ideology, it was working.

It would be an understatement to say that Jitender changed my life, but as Make Love Not Scars grew and started getting media coverage and credibility, he helped me work on my self-confidence. The crank calls would come like clockwork once a week; Jitender would answer them with counter-threats and then chortle at the speed with which the miscreants hung up. Although I was still nervous, I learnt to laugh with him over time. If I couldn't do anything about the situation, I decided that the best way forward was to make light of it. I don't know how or why, but I felt safe. Two months into being slightly successful, I picked up the final death-threat call myself. I told my stalker that he could do whatever he liked because when someone like me gets attacked, people listen, watch and stage protests for justice for me and maybe that was precisely what India needed to create awareness about this cause. Given my background, I know that, were I to be targeted, my family and friends wouldn't alienate me or blame me for becoming an acid-attack victim. The stark reality for most of the survivors was that they were often stigmatised by society and asked, 'What dreadful thing did you do to deserve this?' and other such ignorant questions, which led to survivors being ostracised by their family and friends. As sad as it was, I had enough faith in my family to not go down that route. I was fairly sure that my family would fight for justice and that gave me the confidence to tell this malicious caller that his attempts would only cause him more harm than me. I don't know if he ever really believed this, but I saw it as the upside to being attacked. I never wanted to be a martyr and was petrified, but kept telling myself that some good may yet come of it; perhaps this was my purpose on an existential level. Although horrifying, it was a coping mechanism at the time. I never quite made peace with the notion, but it did help me feel stronger to postulate that my face was not being lost in vain but for a cause. I wasn't going to be persecuted for refusing to marry someone, but at the end of the day it would have still been because I exercised my right to say 'no'.

That night I composed a letter to my loved ones and titled it 'In case of my sudden death'. I never received a call after that however and I had to eventually bid Jitender goodbye. I will always cherish the memories of the big bottle of fresh cow milk he would bring for me from his village and the delicious momos that his wife made as a gift for me.

I had got past the threats and learnt to live with the anxiety. I reconciled to the fact that it was my body's instinctive response to stress. It manifested hard and strong before a television interview or a talk, but I was slowly learning to be more gentle with myself. I was learning to accept the parts of me that brought me down. I still haven't got it right but it's all a journey, innit? On the bright side, Make Love Not Scars was no longer a joke to anyone.

Everyone, including my former self, could see that I was actually in it for the long haul and no longer as fickle as I once was.

12

Rehabilitating the Survivors

AT SOME POINT, ONE IS BOUND TO COME TO A crossroads of sorts. It wasn't my work that was failing me, it was my inability to rehabilitate the survivors successfully that was demotivating me. Slowly but surely, I could see myself getting extremely disheartened and even though I was trying to keep my faith intact, I could see my mojo slipping away.

Was it fair that the reason for my dogged determination and tenacious struggle be completely undermined because India was, in general, a slow-moving entity? Everything with Make Love Not Scars had moved so fast in its one short year of existence that any period of inactivity spooked me. Every lull felt like I was giving up. It is not like I genuinely wasn't working, but there were times when there just wasn't any work. The need still existed, but I was helpless, and there wasn't much that I could actually do. I wanted to do a lot of things but the slow processes for every little thing was slowing me down and getting me down. In the end I could always do my side of the work but I was so dependent on the authorities to see an outcome. I could file for government compensation and watch as the process took years, I could fight for justice and become an old woman by the time we got our next hearing or I could try and make the best use of my own time and take up the responsibility myself.

After a long week of procrastination and contemplation, I had an epiphany one night: a brand-new goal. I wanted to make these girls independent; I was fed up of them running after all the wrong things like money. It wasn't their fault though. NGOs in the past have been known to fund survivors although it made the victims dependent on their largesse. Seeking handouts is bad for anyone. It is the wrong outlook to have on life but the survivors, more than anyone, felt entitled to live on charity for the rest of their lives. They didn't understand one thing though, that this was so not true. It was good if a steady stream of donations kept them afloat for the rest of their lives, but we all knew this wasn't going to happen. I was finding it hard enough to just raise funds for surgeries and legal aid, let alone to feed and provide for the girls. I had made it crystal clear that this wasn't my 'duty'.

So I began to ponder, how could I:

1. Change the mindsets of the girls to make them *want* to be independent?
2. Provide for this independence to actually make it a reality?

It wasn't that no one wanted to work; I had girls who actually wanted to be self-sufficient. The ones that did want to be independent had two issues: the illiterate had to be educated or equipped with a skill that enabled them to be employed and earn a dignified living. The ones that were employable required me to eradicate the social stigma that prevented employers from hiring them. Both tasks in themselves, I realised, that we had ample issues with. I needed a sure-shot, kill-two-birds-with-one stone kind of solution, and the obstacles in my way seemed never-ending. Let's say I managed to eliminate the two problems described above, then the next stage would be even more challenging. How do I cater to the variety of disabilities that afflicted my victims?

I possibly couldn't provide for a generalised employment scheme, as each survivor possessed a different handicap. Most NGOs have to contend with one disability per NGO whereas I was a multi-specialty NGO because not only did I have to deal with disfigurement, but a whole array of disadvantages, all of them inflicted in the cruellest way, and none of them congenital. Visual, auditory, speech-impaired, illiteracy, loss of fingers, and that list went on. It was impossible for me to contact a different NGO to help with a different disability and I came to the conclusion that I had to take on all these disabilities and just get over the fact that I thought I couldn't do something about it. I was livid with myself but knew that I was going to hate myself if I didn't do something, anything. The feeling of inadequacy wasn't going to leave me anytime soon so I decided to start working on it before it ate me alive.

After careful consideration and extreme deliberation, I thought I finally had it. I needed to create a system through which I could be the one creating the job profiles depending on each survivor's need and this could only happen if it was Make Love Not Scars providing the employment itself. I thought to myself, 'Wow genius, easier said than done! You sound like a smart kid but how, in god's name, are you going to pull this off?' Well, I didn't know how I was going to pull it off, but I knew I had to. I didn't have any other option. Conducting campaigns and fundraisers to dole out money to the girls was not my priority and that was a promise I made to myself a while ago. So there had to be something more. As for the girls that didn't want to work and just wanted donations handed to them, I decided not to give up on them either. They had to work, they had to live a dignified life and no tragedy that happened to them was going to change that. I know that all they had was money on their minds, but I was determined to change that gradually. A change in mindset takes time and I just had to make sure that I stocked up on patience.

The idea had been on my mind for a while now, but I had always been terrified of exploring it because it always seemed so much bigger than me. So I sat down and thought of my accomplishments so far; I had never intended to create Make Love Not Scars, not even in my wildest dreams, and if I truly wanted to make a change, it was time to go big or go home. Most people my age dream of the next handbag they wanted to own; all I wanted right now was to own a rehabilitation centre. So how would this rehabilitation centre help me address all the problems that the survivors had? A rehab centre would be a safe haven of sorts, a sanctuary run by the survivors for the survivors. It would provide employment for the more experienced girls who would run the centre and ensure everything ran smoothly. The centre would have various classes that would cater to various disabilities. Braille for the blind, sewing for those who had talent, English classes for everyone and dancing and singing for recreation. Not only would this comfortable environment be a delight for the girls, it would also equip them to go out and conquer the world in the future! The rehab centre would also have dorms for survivors visiting Delhi for treatment. This would cut so many costs for them and they would also be able to get themselves the best treatment possible. The survivors that were employed by the organisation would also be in charge of helping the survivors from out of town and the help would include setting up doctors' and lawyers' appointments, with advice from our medical and legal teams to give them tips and provide counselling on how to overcome such a big tragedy. I honestly couldn't have thought of a better solution and my vision for the future was large, I wanted to establish a bunch of these centres all over India.

So what was the plan of action? I had my idea in place but how was I going to implement it? Whenever I told people about this idea, they endorsed its sheer brilliance, but no one thought it was possible to actualise. I had two options—either I could write a proposal and send it off to corporates and ask them to fund it. Or I could run the biggest campaign of my life and finance it myself. The corporates side of it would take time and a lot of rejection letters before it could actually happen and the campaign side of it would be a huge gamble. So what was I going to do? Both. My philosophy was simple, if I put in the work, there was no reason why this wouldn't work. I just had to hold on to my vision and believe in it even when no one else would. So sit at my laptop I did, that proposal had to be ready by the end of today because I was finally sick of how slowly everything was moving. Tomorrow I was going to start working on the campaign. Wish me luck!

13

The TED Talk That Never Was Just a TED Talk

WHEN I WAS YOUNGER I ALWAYS DREAMT OF SPEAKING at TED. When I was younger, I was made to believe that this could never happen. In late 2015 however, my dream came true.

I was contacted by my former school and invited to speak at their first ever TEDx event. At the first mention of it, I was thrilled. I couldn't believe that someone wanted to hear what I had to say and that too for a full eighteen minutes. I was stoked!

After the initial excitement died down, my best friend Patricia decided to pay me a visit. Patricia was someone who was so close to me that she often presided on everything that I did. She wasn't a good friend, however, because all she ever did was bring me down. Since I was so excited about TED, I didn't really want to see her but she's a persistent guest and I never really have a say about when she chooses to appear. The things she says to me make me go weak in the knees and before I know it, my fingers go numb as well. The first time I sat in on a live interview, Patricia had me breathless. She made me feel so inadequate that my vision slowly started getting blurred. I almost fell off the chair in nervous anxiety and all of this on live television. After this, Patricia shadowed me everywhere, on planes, in the car, while I spoke to people, while I attended events and her new favourite pastime was to pop up just when I had to give a talk on stage.

With time, Patricia was the name I gave to my anxiety. After the death threats episode, I decided to make friends with my anxiety. I believed that if I accepted her as a part of me, she wouldn't have the same control over me. Besides, anxiety sounds pretty bleak, while 'Patricia' sounded more friendly. How can you ever be mad at someone called Patricia, right? Anyway, to my surprise, Patricia didn't involve herself in the talk-writing process that much. I wrote over five drafts and eventually decided to make cue cards of the milestones of my journey and just wing it. On the day of the official talk, I realised Patricia was a persistent bitch. I spent the majority of the time in the bathroom before it was my turn to talk. I ran over my pointers again and again and I was petrified of messing up. I wasn't terrified of making a fool of myself but representing my survivors was important to me. I was doing this for them.

Before I knew it, it was my turn and I was called to present my views. As I mounted the short flight of stairs to the platform, I was handed a little remote control to change the slides on my presentation. I probably shouldn't have worn high heels because as soon as I stepped onto that stage into the blinding spotlight, I started trembling. I couldn't see the audience and it was just me and yes, Patricia. Barely into my first sentence, she got to me and reminded me that I was staring into an abyss; I kept repeating the first line like a stuck record. It was like I was an ant put under a microscope and I couldn't understand what the world was looking at. Plagued by these thoughts, I walked off stage. The organisers urged me to walk back and I couldn't explain to them that I had no control over my mind or my body at this point. I couldn't explain that Patricia had taken over and I was a different person.

Dazed and confused, I walked back and announced to the audience that I suffered from anxiety disorder (probably not the best way to start the first TED talk of your life). It was nerve wracking that even after this confession no one reacted. I thought I was chanting 'concentrate' in my mind but ended up saying it into the mic; I was a nervous, shaky, perspiring mess. The instant I made the announcement though, I felt more in control. I thought that even if I botched this, I always had someone else to blame, Patricia. It suddenly got easier and even though I stumbled, fumbled and was far from articulate, I still finished my talk. I don't know how I did it, but it happened. Everyone clapped, I got off the stage trembling and didn't remember a word of what I had said. Watching a video of the talk would later reveal what a colossal embarrassment I was to myself.

I spent a week dwelling on what a failure I was. I had just the one chance and I had screwed it up big time. Everyone around me tried to tell me that I would get better with time, but I was convinced that there would never be a next time because who would want to listen to an incoherent buffoon? I received a call from a corporate social reasonability head at a major corporate a week and a half into my self-pity spree.

'Hello, is this Ria Sharma?'

The call ended with the executive requesting a meeting and we met exactly three days later. As we sat in a café, the sweet yet stern gentleman proceeded to tell me that they had heard my TED talk and had been trying to contact me for a week. I was shocked to say the least. He said the talk was relatable and hard-hitting (I'm glad someone thought so!) and then he asked me what my dream project would be. I was quick to tell him about my dream of starting a rehabilitation centre, so I rambled on about how it would help the survivors and would be a game-changer in the field. He heard me out and as we said our goodbyes, he asked me to send in a proposal with a concept note and costing. As soon as I got back home, I sent him my proposal which I had previously written and crossed my fingers. A month had passed, and I had forgotten about TED and the corporate who I was sure would never get back to me and that's when it happened. I received a text message from the exec at the corporate and it read, 'Congratulations, your funding has been approved.' The world shook because I couldn't believe how a talk that I thought was so awful could have done this. I guess it's true, one man's meat is another man's poison. Three months later, I launched the world's first rehabilitation centre for acid-attack survivors. I also received three more TED invites.

As I sit in the newly set-up rehabilitation centre at my brand-new desk, I start to contemplate. What would have happened and where would I have been if I hadn't struck on this path? Would I have been working under someone doing something monotonous that I had absolutely no interest in? It's funny how life is capable of showing you where your passion lies; I guess it is up to us to jump at the opportunity. Misha, my best friend from boarding school, had been a blessing through this process. She resided in the UK but decided to return to India to volunteer with the organisation to help me set up the centre. She had seen all my meltdowns, had made numerous to-do lists and was proving to be my anchor in what seemed like a sea of work. We had successfully set up the centre but running it was a whole new ballgame. We realised soon enough that we couldn't do it alone. On a busy Saturday, we had three photoshoots lined up with three different magazines. We had journalists waiting in separate rooms and Misha had brought in volunteers to help. The survivors rushed from room to room giving interviews to separate journalists and I ran around like a headless chicken giving my own interviews. The interns helped translate for one of the magazines.

One of the interns at the centre that day was a curly-haired girl named Tania. I was so overwhelmed that I barely had time to talk to anyone. Mid shoot, I decided to take a break and asked Tania if she smoked, she nodded and we instantly had something to bond over. We walked up to the roof of the office and lit up. As we bonded over that initial cigarette, I would have never imagined that would be the moment that changed the course of my organisation. I learnt that Tania was a burn survivor herself. She used to study in Singapore when, in her second year, her hair caught fire in a freak incident in her kitchen. She spent four months in the hospital, had her entire left ear reconstructed and spent two years of her life wearing a wig after that. She had found Make Love Not Scars on Facebook shortly after the incident and was immediately drawn into helping. She would volunteer online and help with social media content and I didn't even know any of this because Misha was handling this side of things. She had just finished college and had moved back to India and was free for the next few months. Tania struck me as a responsible person and she was easy to make conversation with. Her story also contributed to the fact that we hired her the next day. Four months into Tania's journey with Make Love Not Scars, it was clear that I couldn't function without her. Misha had left shortly after Tania joined and not only did Tania shoulder Misha's responsibilities, she dealt with my emotional baggage as well. It took three glasses of white wine and one night of bonding, countless debates about the Syrian war and the future of the organisation. She had become my best friend and the backbone of the NGO. In the sixth month that Tania had been with us, she told me that she needed to speak to me one morning. I sat down and she told me that she would be leaving at the end of the month. I didn't know this, but she had previously accepted a position working with a start-up in Malaysia. She told me that she would reject it if I needed her to stay. My heart was completely broken but I knew I had to let her follow her dreams. As an employer I wanted to beg her to stay but as a best friend I couldn't get myself to do it. On her last day at the centre I bought three caged birds from a roadside vendor because she often spoke about how she would buy all the birds one day and set them free. To my surprise these birds were frightfully expensive, so I could only afford three. I took her up to the same roof where we first bonded and surprised her with the birds. I told her to free the birds as a good deed to annotate this new chapter in her life. She excitedly opened the cage only to realise that the birds wouldn't fly. She had to pry them out with her hands. The first two birds whooshed up into the sky, the third hit a wall on its first attempt and eventually took off as well. We felt great about ourselves until our Australian volunteer, Alex, enlightened us about how birds reared in captivity would have no survival skills and therefore would not

With Reshma while shooting for #EndAcidSale

Taking a selfie together

New York Fashion Week ramp walk practice with Reshma

Survivors Soni and Anupama at the MLNS rehab centre

With survivors Anju and Meena

The infamous TED talk

Meeting Monica for the first time

TIMES

Bennett, Coleman & Co. Ltd.

TIMESOFINDIA.COM | EPAPER.TIMESOFINDIA.COM

Gritty Vijay Steadies Ship

Scores a patient 59 as India take key 145-run lead P 25

337 visit with ...lan P 24

...s away ...k MH17

Kiev: Rebels looting, wiping out evidence

Ukraine has accused pro-Russian rebels of looting valuables belonging to dead flyers and destroying evidence from the wreckage of MH17. "The terrorists have taken 38 bodies to the morgue in Donetsk," the government said on Saturday. Ukrainian PM Arseny Yatsenyuk also claimed the rebels barred experts from collecting evidence and threatened to detain them. But a CNN crew said it did not see any sign of looting or the rebels tampering with evidence. P 24

...g next to you was hit by a ...niper bullet," said the source. As instructed by the con...oller, the AI pilots tried to ...ntact the Boeing 777 after ... transponder display went ... the radar. The message ...y sent was: "Malaysian 17, ...s is Air India 113. How do ... read?" There was, of ...rse, no response.

...ontinued on P 20

...adaun girls' ...raves under ...nga water...

Acid attack & 43 ops later, she fashions a fresh start

24-Yr-Old Eyes Parson's, But Lacks Funds

Jayashree.Nandi @timesgroup.com

Monica Singh was attacked after she rejected a marriage proposal

New Delhi: Monica Singh's face lights up when she talks about her dream to study fashion marketing at Parson's New School of Design in New York. The 24-year-old's flair for style is evident in how she is dressed — a smart skirt paired with a fitted black blouse, and a scarf stylishly draped around her neck.

What the scarf hides are the bandages from a neck surgery, the 43rd reconstruction procedure she has undergone since a horrific acid attack five years ago. A bulb of acid five hired goons threw on her in Lucknow to avenge a rejected marriage proposal had severely burned her torso and face.

But Monica is an irrepressible optimist. Despite the trauma, the long recovery and the many setbacks, she is full of life. Having got admission to a postgraduate course at Parson's, her energies are focused on raising funds for it. She is looking to get crowdfunding and has posted a YouTube video which tells her story on crowdfunding sites such as indiegogo and has put out a plea for grants on http://makelovenotscars.org, a site for acid attack survivors.

"I can go only if I manage to raise money for my studies," says Monica, who is $50,000 short. Brother Nikhil, 31, currently the only earning member in her family, is her rock.

Monica was in the first year of her undergraduate course in apparel design at the National Institute of Fashion Technology when she was attacked in her home town. After an entire year in hospital in Lucknow and spending close to Rs 30 lakh on reconstruction surgeries, she resolutely returned to Delhi to resume her studies.

Two of Monica's attackers are in custody but three are out on bail. Under the new law passed in April, Monica would have been entitled to compensation from the state government as well as the accused. Unfortunately, the assault on her predates this so she does not stand to benefit.

▶ Continued on P 4

Monica's article in *The Times of India*

Receiving the United Nations Bill and Melinda Gates Global GoalKeeper Award from Priyanka Chopra

MLNS wins Brand of the Year at the CNBC-TV18 Indian Business Leader Award

Standing tall with President Obama, Bill and Melinda Gates

Photos: courtesy Ria Sharma

be able to fend for themselves in the outside world. We basically killed the three little birds; my good gesture had inadvertently become a bird of ill-omen for her and that was probably why I received a call from Tania, four months into her new job, asking if she could come back and work with Make Love Not Scars again. The dead birds were our blessing in disguise; Tania became the CEO of Make Love Not Scars and now I'm afraid I can't remember a time that I ever did anything without her.

14

Kanta: Fighter. Survivor. Superwoman.

EVERYONE THOUGHT SHE WAS A BIT STRANGE. SHE had a menacing voice that gave her lamest jokes a vicious edge. She would walk in with an old photograph and claim it was her. Everyone in the office would crack up with laughter and tell her to stop lying. I was also party to this, not realizing the damage I was causing. She didn't seem to mind though, she would laugh along and even though she was not exactly a picture of feminine grace, she would try to bow her head down, getting all coy, perhaps just to amuse us. I would say she was more of a rambunctious tomboy. The fact that she had already been attacked four times before and would speak of another possible attack with a zen smile, told me how she was more of a man than the men who had done this to her. Women in our country are scared and they have reason to be. This one was feisty, a fearless battle horse with all the scars to show for it.

The contradictions were in abundance because she loved putting on make-up. A couple of days after her surgery, Kanta walked up the two flights of stairs with attendants on either side supporting her as she panted and groaned. I waited for her to walk up the last flight, expecting her to collapse in my arms. One large thigh graft and facial implant and I was sure the spunk had been wiped out. She reached the landing and looked up at me. The first thing I see, isn't the bandage on her face, it's the sparkly pink eye liner she has on. In an instant, I'm a happier person.

In the months leading up to her surgeries, I remember this one night that Kanta was spending at the centre along with another survivor named Anupama.

This was Kanta's first night at the centre and soon to be mine as well. While I was busy at work, anxious about the massive campaign we were launching the next day, Kanta would frequently wander into the room and ask me what I wanted to eat. She had a natural maternal instinct and this may have something to do with the fact that she had two daughters. She would bring hot cups of tea and made the most of the few supplies available in our sparsely stocked kitchen. Whether it was toast with butter or hot samosas from the market nearby, the Kanta that everyone thought had 'half a mind' was a domestic goddess for which no one gave her enough credit. I would like to think she had a rare sense of humour and there was a communication barrier that prevented everyone from understanding her. But I saw a self-sufficient woman, hardened by the constant death threats thrown her way. I had immense respect for her and the fact that she smiled at my dark humour gave me a certain sense of acceptance and put me at ease.

Kanta had separation anxiety and it didn't take me long to sense it. When the clock struck six, she stormed into my office and almost ordered me to spend the night with her and Anupama. When I told her that I had a meeting at seven and would leave at about 9 p.m., she seemed a bit worried by this revelation but didn't pester me although she walked away with a sad face. The attack had left Kanta's bottom lip disfigured, inflated and drooping, due to which I could always see her lower jawbone. She looked perpetually sad. Thanks to some technical difficulties, my 7 p.m. meeting with my website manager stretched longer than any of us expected, and at 2 a.m. we decided to call it a night and deal with our problems in the morning. Aditya, the man in charge of my website, passed out on the sofa-cum-bed in my office and I proceeded to the room where Anupama and Kanta were snuggled up in bed. They both looked so comfortable and I literally had nowhere to sleep, so I gently nudged them and asked if I could crawl into bed between the two of them. They both looked confused at first, then looked thrilled and welcomed me with open arms. It seemed so natural. I got in and they covered me on either side with their individual blankets. Without a word and almost telepathically they joined their pillows even before my head rested on them and formed one unified headrest. Both their hands stroked my arms on either side to soothe me to sleep and in that one moment, I felt loved. I always knew I had a thankless job, but these gestures were enough to remind me why I started on this whole project. I was suffering from a mild cough and tried to be discreet with my bouts of coughing, but even though they were sleeping, my coughs didn't go unnoticed. At one point, I thought I had inadvertently woken up Kanta because she opened her eyes and asked me abruptly whether she should face the other way. I thought my coughing was bothering her because we were lying face to face in close proximity. But the reason she asked me this was about to prove that every interview I gave about social stigma being drilled into the minds of the survivors, was indeed not a figment of my imagination. Her injured teddy bear eyes were wide open and faced me in the dim light and her naturally pouty lips with the exposed lower jaw and crooked teeth then went onto mouth the words: 'I'll turn around so you won't see my face every time you wake up and get scared.' If it's possible to silently cry on the inside, it was happening to me. I was appalled.

In an instant, I found my experience failing me. I was at a complete loss for words for I knew from where those words came. Out of concern for me and my well-being, she had transcended to a place of self-acceptance that was forced onto her by society's insensitivity. Our community had successfully drilled the life lesson of passive acquiescence into a human being with disfigurement, in the worst way possible. I know her words emanated from a space in her mind where she had been made this request before. After silently tearing up for twenty seconds, I raised my hand to stroke her head and said, 'I've eaten food made with your hands, I have been with you all day and now I am willingly sleeping next to you and feel fortunate that you would share this space with me. Sleep freely, I will never fear you.' Kanta's eyes sparkled through the darkness while she gave me a goofy, gummy grin. She fell asleep two seconds later, but her words kept me up all night. At least whatever was left of the night.

I had been so lost, so desensitised, so hard that I had almost forgotten why I had started this enterprise. I had forgotten the sentiment and tonight Kanta reminded me and reinforced my passion. It was this very intolerance by society that was the seed of Make Love Not Scars and my keen interest in the lives of the survivors. Something that I had lost sight of in the daily grind of trying to provide for them. I felt like a mother, so exhausted by the process of motherhood that she had forgotten altogether the anticipation of wanting to have a child. Kanta resurrected my maternal instincts but that wouldn't be the only time.

I woke up the next morning to a hand stroking my shoulder and button eyes staring at me. The second I was fully conscious I realised Kanta was all dressed up and ready to seize the day; she started by asking me what I'd like for breakfast.

15

Wishing for Death on a Bed

AFTER A SPELL IN THE BURNS WARD, ONE GETS INURED to the smell. It's the smell of burning hair amplified several times over and the abortive attempts to eradicate the stench were even more evident. It is definitely not Dettol, but some inexpensive solution, a thin, colourless liquid in a transparent unlabelled bottle, which is obviously highly diluted, given its ineffectiveness, and even if it wasn't, it couldn't possibly mask the miasmic misery. Wasted lives, I cannot help but think to myself. At times I cannot help but be conventional in my thinking because I am but human, bound by my own intellect or, in this case, the lack of it, to have such thoughts. There is so much despair everywhere, how do you escape it? Outside the ward, motionless but conscious bodies lay scattered in the corridor on the floor, swathed in bandages from head to toe (thank god for that!). They just lay there like they had nowhere else to be, nothing else to do but wait. Wait for the moment when this will all end and hope that it will be sooner than later. Until then, helpless relatives and friends mill around trying to battle the odds, screaming for doctors and nurses to attend to their patient. But what can the management even do? The beds are full. Every person in that ward is hanging on by a thread with a slim chance of survival—a few days tops. The ones in the corridor wait for a body to be carried out, signifying that they can now take their turn on the death bed. Such is the very sorry state for everyone involved. Everyone wants to help. But if you stay in a burns ward long enough, you get accustomed to the conditions.

Just as you get used to the squalor and sadness, you get used to beds being emptied and bodies being carried out. You get used to seeing a face but grow wary about getting to know their story, the person, the flesh because they too will soon depart. So eventually you desensitise and attempt to achieve a modicum of normalcy. One develops the right amount of insensitivity. One finds the balance and forges ahead. Instead of getting bogged down by trying to find a way to change things which are not going to change for a very long time, you just help in the best way you can.

In the wake of an earthquake, one is left with nothing but ruins and a sudden and inexplicable loss of life and pain. Nothing can change overnight, so one can only help in any and every way that one knows best. You discover new ways to help. People mend the ruins, rebuild their lives, mourn the dear ones they have lost and concentrate on appreciating the ones that are left. Most importantly, people realise that they have no option but to renovate.

Where there once was a building, now lies a pile of rubble. Slowly and steadily, the rubble is removed, the plot remains barren for a while. Small shrubs and trees sprout through the cracks in the debris and eventually one day, when the city has stopped mourning, a new foundation is laid. That foundation, over a period of time, turns into a new building, bigger and better this time, and earthquake-proof as well. Only when one is completely ruined can one come back stronger.

In a situation of crisis, one sticks around and stays strong because otherwise one would be doing more harm than good. I stop to smoke a cigarette before I enter the hospital for the fiftieth time. It never gets easy; the smell already seeps into my skin and I haven't even walked in yet. I look at the entrance of the hospital, it is not a busy day. There are only about fifty people lying around in the lawn of the small garden outside the entrance. I see about twenty of them swaddled in gauze; it doesn't seem to be a hectic day. I have dressed down hoping to stay under the radar and pass like a ghost without attracting any attention. I don't want anybody to think that I come from any sort of privileged background. I am scared; I was scarred a long time ago but this place always gives me the chills. Just a few feet away is the doorway to hell, where people just sit around with no faces, no features, no body parts and under red body cages. Burns require utmost care and although one doesn't stop to think about this, wearing clothes in such a situation would be agonising. Hence, body cages. A dome-like structure over the patients which is then draped with a red blanket. All the blankets at this hospital are red, like beacons of warning. Walk away; raise this screen at your own peril, you will never be the same again if you do not heed this warning. Not only do the blankets talk, the walls do, too. They speak of the things that they have seen. Fathers who have lost their daughters; daughters who are beyond recognition but loved nonetheless. These walls seem to want to tell me about all the girls who didn't really care about losing their faces because they could barely breathe. They have heard people screaming in the middle of the night with pain, shock and trauma; their shrieks go unnoticed because that's the norm here. Everyone is used to it. A day in the life of a tile in the burns ward; I pity the tile for having such a life; I pity the blanket for bearing the brunt of someone's hate and violence. I pity the people that are left alive in mourning and considered the departed as lucky. You can hear the sighing of the wind however—a different kind of sound. Twenty women in the ward simultaneously gasping for air and if you listen to it long enough, mixed with the sound of a beep here and a beep there of the intermittent machinery, it synchronises into a dirge. A song of utter sadness and misery, the only melody is in the hope produced by the togetherness and affinity of the people who are caring and supporting these hapless victims. I am not alone; the girl in the bed next to me sounds just like me and I sincerely hope that she will still be there when I wake up in the morning.

My cigarette burned down quite quickly; I wish it had lasted longer; I wonder whether I should light up another one. My driver knows the drill; he is not blind and knows exactly where we are. I am not just scared but much more than that—I am petrified. It's not so much about the things I'm about to see, I'm fairly seasoned by now. I am worried about how much more damaged I could get. How many nights is it going to take for me to recover this time? Everyone assumes I am wholly immune now and I don't bother to disillusion them. The truth, however, will always be different. Like the women on the ventilators that whistle a different tune, I find myself living a lie sometimes. Their breaths sing of hope when I know they are suicidal. The fact that they breathe doesn't signify that they want to, but they still breathe for the people around them. I, too, sing a different tune to satisfy the people around me because how long can someone listen to my tale of woe? I'm not even a survivor. I was never entitled to suffering, I wasn't attacked. Therefore, I suffer in silence, wondering how long the effects of this ward will haunt me this time. How many nights will I wake up with a silent, anonymous pang of fright and whisper, 'I'm stronger than this,' and put myself back to sleep. I want to know what my recovery speed will be this time. It has been getting easier however and although it still haunts me, it is manageable. I have never been lachrymose, so that's a definite advantage that I can boast of. Misery, however, really does hit me and I can boast of that as well, because if it didn't get to me the way it does, I wouldn't be doing this today. I wouldn't want to help if I didn't take misery as seriously as I do.

I need to go in now, no amount of procrastination is going to change my fate and while most don't know what their fates hold, I know mine. In this moment and the few that follow, until I exit the hospital, I know exactly what I'm destined for. It's surprising that even when one knows that something bad is imminent, nothing in the world can prepare one for it. I mean if I knew an earthquake was on the cards, I would evacuate immediately. But right now, I am consciously and deliberately walking into doom, just hoping that I can change someone else's.

I get out of the car and make my way to the main entrance of the hospital that houses only three burns wards. At least this specific branch does. The people that once looked like ants from my car window in the distance, now have clearer faces. I can see their features, their faces sorrowful as they echo the song of misery. It starts at the doorway and really never ends because it gets seared into the hippocampus. My stomach churns like I have had two large neat vodka shots and I feel the burning in the pit of my soul. I walk in; chaos. Stretchers, flesh, blood, more stretchers, nurses hurrying around in uniforms that are too impeccably white for their surroundings. Groaning, moaning, hustle, bustle; there is nothing organised about it. The yelling, crying and pleading fall on deaf ears but the walls are listening, capturing, documenting and recording them like dirty little secrets. There is a massive clock in the lobby, it shows us that time is ticking; someone is breathing their last somewhere, we need to value our time. We need to be more thankful; the clock taunts me and I ignore it because, 'I'm stronger than this.' I speak to no one because I know the drill and know the exact bed number and I know how to get there without asking anyone. Dressed down, I'm a spectre that can go wherever I like. I try to stay focussed on the movement of my own two feet, but it is impossible. A girl lies in a corner, half-bandaged and that's never a good thing. She is burnt and I'm worried that she is going to catch an infection. But you can't save everyone, so I continue walking. I wish I were Mother Teresa, maybe then I could save this victim; but she might not be an acid-attack survivor and if I don't stick to that classification, there's nothing to stop me from volunteering to help cancer patients. I feel the desolation and misery which compels me to reach out and help, but I resolutely clamp down on the urge. I don't want to induce fake hope and must stick to the field I know best where I know I can truly help. I walk past her like a battle-scarred veteran. She didn't bother to ask for help and I walk past her still thinking about that infection that could cost her her life. I want someone to pick her up on one of the million stretchers; why aren't they picking her up? They say the safest place is a hospital, but this seems like a breeding ground for infections. Are they actually low on stretchers? I just saw like a billion.

'Just focus on your feet, Ria, keep walking. Don't look up, look at the ground, try not to step on anyone and walk,' my inner voice whispers and I counter it, 'How can I not look? There are bodies everywhere; there's something so intriguing about pain, but then again curiosity did kill the cat. So, keep walking.'

I am still young; my parents think I am a child. I don't even know how to pay the electricity bill, my dad always did it and in college, my flatmate, Fran, held that responsibility. The point though? Nothing, I just had a weak moment and that's normal. Getting my mind back into the game, I promise myself a large glass of wine as an incentive as soon as this is done. I try to shake off the image of the infection-prone girl and march down the dimly-lit corridor to the ward. It's a sunny day outside and a few windows exist along the narrow room, but even the sun is wary and refuses to shine here. I reach the ward where the ward-boy sitting outside has seen me often enough to recognise me although he doesn't know my name; I proceed to remove my shoes without any signal from him. I know the drill and he knows I know it too. I quietly slip off my flip-flops that were a part of my underdressed attire; even if someone stole them, I wouldn't mind. However, I'm paranoid about walking barefooted outside and stepping on something I shouldn't. If I had planned ahead, I would have worn Converse. The more the laces, the more the time to dawdle and postpone doom. If I hadn't left home in such a hurry, I would have remembered. It is just that Sanjana called in such a panic that I rushed down to see what was happening for myself. She said that she had a case for me that involved an attack on not one, not two, not three, not four or five, but six people all at once. For the life of me I couldn't even understand what that meant, so I had to have a look for myself. Bed number twenty-one was my destination. The bed was situated in the second ward, the second one on my right as soon as I entered the corridor. That was my silver lining; I wouldn't have to cross too many people to get to the survivors, except the ones that were laid out on the sides of the aisle of course. Okay, it is time to be strong and just walk in. 'Strong, strong, strong, strong, I'm stronger than this. Chant and walk, chant and walk. Wine, cigarette, wine.' When I enter, I'm not the strong one—they are—I just have to be immune because I have seen this pain far too many times, but this is their first.

Baaaammmmm ... first bed on my right has someone so disfigured I know she's never going to make it.

16

A Family Tragedy

I'M NOT USING THE TERM 'DISFIGURED' TO REALLY talk about her appearance, well that too, but assessing the damage, her case doesn't look promising. I think she knows that as well. She's silent. I think she has to be—everything is burnt. She doesn't have eyelids to blink (why is that not bandaged?)—questions everywhere, answers nowhere in sight. I don't think she can swallow either, her neck seems non-existent. Is this a fresh case? Because she really hasn't been bandaged at all. She's not even in a body cage and there's no sign of the red blanket either. Wait, I spoke too soon, bed-on-my-right, I spot a body cage, a red blanket and I see a head peeping out of the top of the cage; it's staring at me. Should I say 'hi'?

'No, Ria. No distractions, go to bed number 21.'

The beds are partitioned by walls, for good reason too—it ensures that the patient doesn't see the other burn patients; furthermore, these patients are also kept away from mirrors so they don't really know what they look like. These measures are in place to avoid exacerbating their trauma and suffering. If they catch a glimpse of their fellow inmates or their own reflection, the severity of their situation would dawn on them and then they would not feel lucky about the bed they are given, one that they had to fight for in the first place due to the lack of availability. The girl in the body cage seems very docile, she's not panicked; I don't see pain on her face or the presence of misery around her cage, she seems like she is at peace. Perhaps she has been here for a while and had made peace with her situation; it's refreshing and I'm impressed by her calm fortitude. I both want and don't want to know the extent of her burns which is confusing, conflicting, intriguing and mysterious. I want to peep under the blanket and find out more, but that's how the cycle starts before it completely takes over. I know that the more I see, the worse my insomnia will get; but it's like a drug. I HAVE TO KNOW MORE. I stop myself. I know she will tell me what happened but it's actually none of my business, and I need to focus on why I came here. The girl on my left without the body cage and bandages can't see me, I feel safe. I think she's blind; okay I'm sure she's blind. I feel awful; she's completely, irreversibly and devastatingly burnt. I wish her to have the release of death and that's my honest prayer for her. Her father, who, going by his clothes, seems to be a construction site labourer of some sort, sits by her bedside. He appears to be all cried out. A white stubble has taken over his dark complexion. His hands are calloused and his feet are cracked and muddy. He should get away from her; she's not bandaged, and he could give her an infection. I wish him a short memory. Caught between the first two beds on either side, I'm consumed with wanting to know more. Which way do I go? I go straight.

I enter my girl's sequestered cubicle type thing. She is sitting bolt upright in the bed, leaning her arms on top of the cage that covers the lower half of her body. For an instant, I think she's wearing a white top, but as I get closer, I realise it is actually bandages that swathe her torso making it seem like she is in a three-quarter sleeved top. She's a plump little thing; half her face is burnt, and still in the 'hope phase'. I put on my brave face. I'm ready to start being a ray of hope now; it's time to put my own shit aside and sparkle; it's time to reach out and help. The buildings have collapsed; there's nothing to do but dig into the rubble, grab a survivor's hand and haul them out. The minor scratches I may get on the way mean nothing, time to pull ... pull someone out of misery. The rescue mission has begun, but I think I spoke too soon—something I seem to do a lot; it really needs to stop.

I get closer; her father is on a chair by her bed. Another woman tends to her; she's definitely a relative, not a nurse.

Urvi looks up at me mid-sentence; she's not my average survivor. Her right eye is badly damaged and she can barely open it, but she glances up nonetheless. She makes being in that much pain look easy. Squinty-eyed, Urvi asks me who I am in a confident and chirpy tone. I think I'm more shocked now. I look at her and query, 'Urvi?' which is all I'm able to say because I'm suddenly tongue-tied and inarticulate. When she confirms that that is indeed her name, my power of speech is miraculously restored and I tell her who I am, hoping that my reputation to help girls in her situation has preceded me and that she may find comfort in my presence. She is completely unimpressed; she has the kind of attitude that says that she could do this with or without me and I like that. It makes me feel more comfortable because this way, even if I disappoint she won't care. I try to tell her again exactly what it is that I do, but she still doesn't look greatly impressed. Urvi's father, on the other hand, is all ears by now because he knows the plight that they are in and is wholly aware that his family could use another helping hand. Urvi, however, doesn't give her father a chance to talk or anyone for that matter and launches into her story. For the life of me, I couldn't take her seriously. I should have, the situation was dire; she was serious but oh so cute. She wasn't talking about her pain but about the person who did this to her. Her body language resembled that of a lioness, with confidence embedded in every action, a lioness ready to battle anyone to protect her cubs.

The stage was set. Urvi donned a red sari with a fluffy gold border. Her lustrous, dark eyes smouldered with *kajal* in the most beautiful way. A multicoloured garland of flowers around her neck. An average-looking girl, but with eyes that gleamed expressively. She holds her face in her hands the way any cheesy photographer would picture an Indian bride. She was stereotypical perfection. I look into those eyes and see the dreams of a seventeen-year-old girl who cannot wait to start her married life. Her parents look proud in the background. The same man who sits at her bedside with burns on his arms and his forehead bunched up in wrinkles actually looks very different in the happy family portrait; she's obviously the apple of his eye. The bridegroom is from an affluent family, at least as affluent it can get for the lower middle class. He wears a garland of fifty-rupee notes around his neck and appears a tad cocky; his eyes don't shine as brightly as Urvi's and he even appears slightly inebriated in the picture. I look at Urvi's *kohl*-smudged eyes in the picture as she shows me more photographs of her wedding day. I look at her eyes now. There's no *kohl* but the undamaged eye still sparkles. She points to her husband and unleashes a string of profanities in Hindi. I can tell she's no doormat and the other patients in the ward wish they spoke with the same courage. Urvi was tortured by her husband and in-laws for two years: they beat her and kept her hostage for dowry. Finally, in the dead of the night, Urvi took a leap of faith and escaped to her maiden home. She wasn't sure if she would still be welcome there, but she knew her father was a kind man who had reared her with love and pride—unlike many other Indian parents of that milieu who rejoice at the birth of a boy and bewail the arrival of a daughter. That fateful night, Urvi's father welcomed her back with open arms. The next day, her husband arrived, with all guns blazing and demanded she return home with him. Urvi, peeking through a crack in the door, watched as her father politely urged the man to go home because his daughter was not to be an object of his misogynistic abuse. But when her husband hurled insults at her father, Urvi crashes open the door and in no uncertain terms tells him to get lost. I was thoroughly impressed by this redoubtable feminist. Her father sighs and buries his head in his hands as she recounts that part chuckling at the vivid memory.

The boy did indeed go back empty-handed, but returned to Urvi's home the next day. Urvi ran away from her demons in the dead of the night and the very same demons crept up on her in the dead of the night. While Urvi, her parents, her two younger sisters and her six-month-old nephew lay sound asleep under a starry night on the roof of their house, they were awoken to the burning of their bodies and screams at 2 a.m. Urvi's husband had doused not only her but her entire family including her six-month-old nephew in highly concentrated acid. The family was rushed to Delhi for urgent and specialised treatment.

Urvi's father refuses treatment, saying the burns on his arm are minor compared to his daughter's condition. A humble man, I want to give him a hug, but then he might think it's inappropriate. Urvi continues to vilify her husband and assures me that I shouldn't worry because she is going to put him behind bars. I don't know how to tell her that she's saving me. Instead of me bolstering her morale, she instils hope in me. When I ask about the rest of the family, I am told that Urvi's mother and youngest sister along with the baby stayed back in Meerut due to lack of funds. I am told that Urvi's other sister is in this hospital. I want to meet her immediately and check to see if she shares the same fighting spirit as her older sister. The doctor arrives and gives me an update on her situation, I don't believe what I'm hearing but I listen to him anyway. He tells me her injuries are grave and that she may not make it. I sneer at him in my head; this man is obviously not a doctor. Is he talking about the same Urvi who is ready to kill her attacker at the moment? Cute, feisty, squinty-eyed Urvi? He tells me she needs blood, I put out a tweet as soon as he informs me. In the next five minutes I have a blood donor, that's one problem down. My brain goes into overdrive; the lack of misery has given me the mind space to actually find a very proactive solution. I need to shift her to a private hospital, yes, I'm going to get her out of here. That's my plan.

I have arranged for blood and now I need to bid the family farewell and go pester some private hospitals into treating Urvi. The younger sister completely slips my mind but just as I'm about to exit the ward, I enquire about her. The father offers to take me to her on our way out. I smile and tell Urvi not to worry, before I leave. She assures me that she's not worried at all. The other woman in the cubicle appears to be a relative who is here to provide moral support to the family, but there's something odd about her behaviour. I don't have the time to analyse what it is that's actually odd. I make my way to the place where I had left my footwear; all of a sudden the gloom of the ward lifts and I'm full of hope. Urvi's father trails behind me and we both put on our shoes. The guard smiles at me in recognition and we proceed towards the exit which is through the next ward and past the main lobby that houses the big clock. I stride confidently now, down the 'hopeless' corridor; I'm hoping Urvi's father behind me is impressed by my knowledge of the layout of this hospital. I don't think I have ever navigated these floors with such confidence before. I have a quick chat with the walls as I daydream and power-walk; I tell them it's a good day to be them. Just when the walls were about to respond, I notice Urvi's father isn't behind me anymore. I turn around, but he's nowhere to be seen. I retrace my steps to find him and almost tripped. I look down to see Urvi's father down on his haunches. I'm startled to see him bent down and tending to the girl I saw earlier. The girl I wanted to help but couldn't; the girl who could catch an infection on the dirty floor of the hospital; the girl who wasn't on a gurney.

He looks up at my puzzled face and explains, 'Madam, *yeh hamari doosri bitiya*, Usha.'

17

Urvi's Fight for Life

I TAKE A SECOND TO PROCESS WHAT I HAVE JUST heard and seen; then I crouch next to the girl. Panic sets in. She could have an infection, she could die. Why isn't she properly bandaged? And where's the STRETCHER! In a second I transform into a strange combination of a virago and headless chicken; I run to the lobby and look at the clock. It's ticking, it's taunting me. She's on the filthy floor ... infections ... she's not covered with protective gauze ... WHERE IS THE STRETCHER!? I grab a ward boy who is passing by, wheeling an empty gurney, and demand that he come with me AT ONCE. I'm the cynosure of all eyes as he argues with me, deeply resenting this hijack. I'm shrieking now and wishing that I hadn't dressed down and had worn make-up so he would recognise my privileged background and take me more seriously. I grab his stretcher and soon a full on tug-of-war is in progress when we are interrupted by the head doctor. The doctor is alarmed that I'm going to burst into tears and tells the ward boy to go with me. The sullen ward boy moves at a snail's pace, but I don't care ... infections on my mind, I chivvy him along because he seems to have developed heavy feet. We are both behaving like children right now. I am told that Usha is all of fourteen years. The father welcomes the sight of the gurney the way a person stranded on a desert island would hail his rescue boat. Usha is unconscious now; she never asked for help, nevertheless I make sure she is put on the stretcher. I love God right now because he is saving me from a lot of regret. I am glad that the girl in the corridor is Urvi's sister. There are no available beds in the hospital, but she's on a stretcher, the ward boy is sulking but the girl's father's eyes gleam with anticipation and hope. Usha is unconscious, but not for long if I have any say in the matter. I leave the hospital with a promise to return in two hours. I'm leaving the hospital now, but I don't think I'll ever have a problem coming back here again. I get into the car and don't light a cigarette; by now even my driver can tell things have changed. I skip the glass of wine; I don't need an incentive anymore.

I worked late into the evening looking for ways and means to help the family. The fact that Usha had been discharged in the state that she was in made a few things abundantly clear to me. It was obvious that beds in government hospitals were reserved for those who were knocking on death's door. The ones that had a fighting chance, didn't stand a chance to secure a bed and by the time the hospital would admit them, they were no different from their counterparts who only got these beds as their death beds. I started consulting lawyers about using the Supreme Court order which stipulated that all government and private hospitals must provide treatment to acid-attack survivors free of cost, including surgeries, medication and even perishables like food. The judgement was beautiful—it was crystal clear and there was just no ignoring it. It stated that hospitals could not even cite 'shortage of beds' as a reason to withhold admission for an acid-attack victim. It was right there, in black and white, with a stamp from the Supreme Court of India, the highest legal authority in the country. I felt a little relieved and knew exactly what my next course of action was going to be. I had never done it before and if it failed, I could be responsible for the death of two girls. But to my mind, they were going to die anyway if I left them where they currently were.

I telephoned the family and asked them to opt for voluntary discharge. A voluntary discharge indicates that the patient is fully aware that she is being discharged against the advice of her doctor. I then arranged for an ambulance to convey both the girls to a hospital. It is one of India's largest privately run hospital chains with some of India's best doctors working round the clock to save lives. I picked this hospital because, even though most private hospitals didn't have burns wards, it had a burns ICU. I'm sure that's not the technical term for it, but it looks a little like an ICU—oh well, more like a room that only housed burn patients in a quarantined environment to minimise the risk of infections. That was good enough for me. I asked the survivors to meet me there. On their arrival, I knew it was going to be an uphill battle, so I decided to approach the situation with tact and a strategy. Yes, I am the new-age con-artist. I instructed them to keep mum about the cost of the treatment and to only answer illness-related questions. The girls were ushered into the emergency room in true cinematic fashion, on gurneys, with doctors hollering instructions. What a change from the government hospital!

I let the doctors do their job, assess the injuries and come up with a course of action. As soon as they were ready, the doctors came to speak to me. Both girls were in dire need of immediate medical intervention; failure to do so would most definitely result in their deaths. His words, not mine. I nodded vigorously and agreed with everything he said. He ended his protocol rigmarole with, 'Okay then, please hurry up and complete the procedures at the billing department because we really have to admit them asap.' I headed to the billing department, which in this case was the desk outside the emergency room. I told them about the Supreme Court order and placed the printed version which I had so kindly even highlighted, in order to not waste their time, and mine, of course. Their faces drooped and they told me to wait. I waited, patiently, for two whole hours before my patience ran out. I strode into the emergency room to speak to the doctor who was ensconced at his desk chatting with his colleagues. He appeared to not have a care in the world ... until I walked in that is. Before I could speak, another hospital employee materialised beside me and asked me to hand over my phone. As a reflex, I gave him my phone and continued to make my way to the doctor's desk. In the short two seconds that my phone was taken from me, I realised that this was totally weird. I made a quick U-turn into the room where the gentleman had taken my phone and found him rifling through my phone. I was gobsmacked and snatched my phone from him; he was shocked and scared and rightly so. I walked out slamming the door behind me, this time determinedly staying on my course to the doctor's desk. I announced that what they were doing was illegal and then I walked right out. My hands were trembling and I genuinely felt outnumbered.

I wanted my parents to come to this hospital and take over. I wanted someone, anyone, to tell this hospital that they had no right to go through my phone and that refusing admission to these girls was tantamount to breaking the law. I immediately drove to the nearest police station. If no one took me seriously at the hospital, no one took me seriously at the police station either. My frustration had reached a peak and I felt a weird sense of vulnerability. If something happened to these girls because of me, I would never forgive myself. I sat at the police station across a man who obviously thought I was a mutinous child, and even worse, a woman. It really wasn't helping my case. They hoped to mollify me into not filing a complaint and that's when it happened. All those feelings, the anger and the frustration broke through in the form of sobs. Yes, I bawled out loud like a baby, attracting attention and guess what? It scared the cops. Stating the law, threatening to sue, citing the grave urgency of the situation, nothing had worked! But in one second, my dreadful yowling had penetrated. They handed me tissues, a glass of water and the ACP started to talk to me kindly. After hearing me out, he sent a constable with me to the hospital. This time, although I walked in with puffy eyes, I felt more authoritative. The constable explained to the hospital that I was on the right side of the law and that it would be in their best interests to treat the victims. Within the next fifteen minutes, I completed the registration documents, admitted Usha and Urvi and ran out of the hospital with a promise to their father that everything was going to be all right now. I couldn't believe the day I had had. To implement laws that were essentially the rights for these survivors (and for the entire nation) had taken a great deal out of me. I couldn't imagine what was happening to the girls that didn't have an NGO fighting for their rights; the humiliation, insensitivity and sheer indignity that the women had to face (with no face) to claim what was rightfully theirs. I was harrowed and emotionally drained, but I was happy that the girls were not going to die ... not today.

Urvi and Usha had made friends with all the staff at the hospital, they were recovering well two months after their attack. They were in adjacent beds and it was baffling to think that one of these girls was deemed fit for discharge at the last hospital. Urvi had created a special bond with her doctor who was the head of plastic surgery at the hospital. Dr Kuldeep was a true gem. He had the right amount of sensitivity. His partner, Dr Shaheen, was the practical one and they complemented each other very well. Over the last two months, everyone had taken to the girls and would do everything in their power to keep them smiling. It wasn't easy being incarcerated in a hospital for two months. Dr Kuldeep had given special instructions to the catering crew to provide eggs for Urvi because she liked them so much and they would also bring her fish every now and then. Urvi had lost so much weight, which was a matter of concern to the medics, but even so her fighting spirit remained indomitable as was her cheerful grin. The girls were to be discharged in a month's time or even sooner as their recovery was coming along swimmingly. I was informed that they were eagerly looking forward to going back home. Even though Urvi would talk about getting justice the second she was allowed to leave the hospital, the situation was a little different when she was about to fall asleep. Most nights Urvi would wake up in a puddle of tears and panic, screaming, 'He's here, he's going to do it again. He's here to get me again.' The nurses would rush to her bedside and assure her that there was no 'he' here. Her attacker was stalking her thoughts, lurking in the shadows and attacking her sanity every night. I couldn't even begin to imagine that level of PTSD. The night was Urvi's enemy and even though I could get her the best treatment possible, it was going to be a long while before she made peace with her demons. Her body was recovering, but her soul was still convalescent. I was convinced that the only way to deal with this would be to take it one step at a time. I had a plan for her once she got discharged and it included a lot of therapy.

A week before the girls were due to be discharged, I received a call at 3 a.m. Luckily my insomnia was keeping me up most nights, so it's not like I was rudely woken up. The minute I picked up this call, however, I came fully awake. At 2.35 that morning, Urvi had passed away. My heart crashed to the ground and my throat closed up. I felt a paralysing stillness take over my body. The world went quiet and dark and just when I was about to succumb to a full-blown nervous breakdown, the voice at the other end of the line said, 'Can you please come and sign the death certificate? Her father is in shock and unresponsive.' For a second I had forgotten my role; I had forgotten that in times like these it is not my place to be still or shocked. I said, 'Yes, of course,' and rushed to the hospital in my night suit. I reached the hospital to find Urvi's bed screened off from Usha's. She was fast asleep and blissfully unaware that when she woke up her sister would no longer be in the adjacent bed. Although I envied her ignorance at that moment, I felt sorry for what she would have to deal with the next morning. I went to the nurse's station which was a panoptic island amidst the beds. Her father sat silent and stared unseeingly at the table. The minute he saw me, he raised his hands in a silent query. He couldn't process this calamity, not after staying by his daughters' bedsides for the past three months, hoping against hope. He just couldn't understand what had happened. I wanted to offer solace and condolences, but I couldn't understand it either. It is true: death can never be understood, only felt. It is also inexplicable and indescribable; it just is. It is the ultimate truth, the last chapter, the end of hope and the beginning of eternal mourning. He looked at me and finally heaved a huge sigh before he broke down into the great silent sobs of a parent who has lost a child. I was helpless.

I wanted to do my best to try and ease his pain, so I decided to complete all the formalities that surrounded the death of a patient. I didn't know what these formalities were, but I was kindly guided by the staff. I was taken to Urvi's bed and I was told that we were to examine her body so I could sign the death certificate. I didn't quite understand what there was to 'examine', but went along with it nevertheless. I wasn't aware at the time that the first time one sees a dead body is never going to be the last time one sees it; it will haunt one forever, stalking one's nightmares and innermost thoughts. The stillness of her lifeless body was surreal; her nose was stuffed with cotton and her eyes were closed. A voice inside my head suggested I violently shake her back to life, but the voice of reason reminded me of my role. The nurse went over the different body parts which she said I had to see in order to sign. After scrutinising the corpse, I was finally allowed to sign the papers. It is funny how a live human body can channel energy, joy and happiness, but when the life leaves a body, all it leaves behind is the body. So, what was the purpose of this body? The body would then be taken for post-mortem and finally buried that evening. I told her father I had finished all the paper work and would arrange for whatever else needed to be done. I spoke to the police that had come to the hospital to record the death and I left. I left the hospital but Urvi never left me. I left the hospital but Urvi never did.

I could try and explain how I felt for the next two weeks or how I feel now as I write this but there's nothing to write. There's no need for anyone to feel the way I did, the way her father felt, the way Usha felt, no one should have to know what that feels like. Urvi's death did teach me an invaluable lesson that true misery is when someone closes their eyes for the last time. Before that we hope and attempt to rebuild like we do after an earthquake. I thought I had seen anguish in the wards, but in Urvi's death I finally saw the true face of despair. We were later told that Urvi's body could eventually not handle the trauma it had been through. She finally succumbed to a cardiac arrest.

Usha remained in the hospital for the next two weeks. The day that she was to be discharged, I dropped in to say goodbye. The nurses had all chipped in and bought Usha a massive teddy bear as a parting gift. Usha left the hospital without her sister but with a new companion and a full life to look forward to.

18

The Case of the Fake Michael Kors

WE WALK INTO THE DOCTOR'S OFFICE—THE MAN IN the chair across me is one of India's best. Sanjana is next to me, extremely nervous. For survivors, meeting good doctors is like meeting celebrities and surgeries themselves are like receiving the best gift ever. Much like cosmetic-surgery junkies, the girls actually wait eagerly for months to go under the knife and get operated on by one of the best. Unlike cosmetic-surgery junkies, however, these girls actually need these surgeries not in order to enhance existing features but to actually rebuild them. The doctor hasn't even started speaking yet and Sanjana is already fizzing with excitement (on the inside). Her one and only eye is sparkling and if this man doesn't start talking soon, I have a feeling she's going to faint. On the other hand, I smell a whiff of arrogance, even contempt. I personally don't believe one has the right to be conceited no matter what one has achieved in life. As soon as I twigged onto his antics, my opinion of him plummeted. But I hold my tongue because of Sanjana. He has already decided he can treat me like a child because he's all of sixty years old and I'm just twenty-one. I think my formal attire despite the lack of grey hair on my head rankles somehow. I'm used to ageism by now so his opinion doesn't really bother me. What is actually getting my goat right now is the fact that he is wasting my time. He isn't even taking a look at Sanjana and pretends to be busy on his laptop, although this is a paid appointment.

Eventually, Dr white-hair-and-long-moustache decides to give us the time of day and asks Sanjana to climb aboard the examining chair so he can have a closer look. Sanjana unveils and he starts spouting fancy medical jargon while his secretary diligently jots down everything at the speed of lightning like his life depends on it. It's Greek to both Sanjana and myself, so I ask him, very politely, to translate it into English. He smirks. I can read his mind now, '... check out this little girl who has walked into my office in her skinny jeans; let me quickly jump at this opportunity to put her in her place.' He proceeds to painstakingly explain the procedure he has in mind in the most condescending manner possible, like I'm not just guilty of extreme youth, but have cognitive and comprehension problems to boot. It must have been a daily ritual for him to belittle others to reinforce his ego; and all the while he talks, I keep thinking that if I can absorb his quota for the day of being mean and nasty, I may save another person some humiliation. So, I patiently listen and collect my good karma.

By the end of the appointment I realise there's absolutely no point whatsoever to argue with this pompous man. He is someone who has made a name for himself and pots of money. In an attempt to appeal to the non-existent humanity in him, I ask him if he can make some sort of a concession so Sanjana could save some of her funds for her next surgery. I have done this before and doctors have said 'no' and that's completely fine by me. But what's not fine by me is what he proceeds to say next. He is perhaps mortified at my audacity to ask for a 'discount' when all I was actually asking was that he offer his skilled hands for some charity. At this point, however, I actually feel like I have asked my father for a Ferrari. He looks disgusted and for the first time, I feel like I'm going to cry just a little bit. His eyes pierce through my very soul as he looks disparagingly at me like I'm the spawn of Satan; and I'm freaking out inside, I swear! Strong, confident and outspoken Ria has left the building; I'm reduced to a timid little girl who wishes her mommy or daddy would come to save her from the big bad wolf. Even though I'm losing it in my head right now, I think I'm maintaining a cool exterior. Thank God I'm seated and he can't see my knees shaking. Just when I think he's going to open his mouth to say something vituperative, he tells me to put my purse on his table. Without a second thought, I obey, I mean where could he possibly be going with this?

When he picks up my purse, I actually want to snatch it back because I think he's going to go through its contents. My bag in his hands is a funny picture because he's sixty something years and here he was clutching a girl's bag and let's face it! That's just weird.

I take a second to giggle to myself; I still don't know where he's going with this.

He strokes the bag once and stops when his hand touches the logo. Oh, would Michael Kors be mad at his touch right now? and that's when it hit me: Jesus! He's hinting at Michael! Literally the only designer bag I own, gifted to me by very cute grandparents who thought I should carry something decent-looking. Now Dr white-hair actually opens his mouth: '*Toh aap itna mehnga bag lekar ghoom rahe hai aur mujh se surgery ke paise ke bheek mangne aaye hai*?' Okay, now I'm shell-shocked, I actually don't know what to say. A pang of anxiety makes its way up my throat and deprives me of speech.

The silver lining? I'm in a hospital so in case I actually break into a full-blown panic attack, I'll get immediate help.

I am cudgelling my brain for an appropriate comeback, but I'm wishing he had said that in English because my Hindi repartee is slightly weak. I'm also wondering whether I should reply in Hindi or in English and if replying in English would only serve in strengthening his case. This man doesn't even know me and he doesn't know the story behind that bag; he doesn't know that I barely own any designer things. The bag he so calmly stroked happened to be a precious and thoughtful gift and he had managed to taint it as an object by which to define my work and lifestyle.

I would have had to save up to buy that bag, but that's not even the point; I could have owned a billion bags like that and yet asked him to be a part of some good will, right? While these thoughts and mixed feeling flooded my mind, he took my silence as another opportunity to further confuse me. This time he chooses to speak in English and I'm relieved that I can at least respond with coherent sentences and lace it with the right degree of sarcasm.

'So, you wear Rs 50,000 on your arm, but can't afford to pay for this surgery?' Now I'm not confused. He's wrong; that bag doesn't cost fifty thousand, it's about ten thousand, number one.

Number two, this man has officially gotten on my nerves.

I open my mouth to say something useful and the only thing that comes out is, 'Sir, for your information, that bag is a fake. I bought it from Bangkok.'

JUST GREAT, RIA! Just when I thought I would say something coherent in a language of my choice, that's what I choose to say? Very mature, very factual and very hard-hitting. He is confounded. I just told him I'm toting a fake bag and I think we both just realised the shallow nature of our conversation. He chuckles softly, I giggle and Sanjana cannot comprehend what's going on. The secretary who's obviously paid to keep a straight face doesn't know if he's invited to join in the humour of the situation so he satisfies himself by just looking confused.

All in all, things just got extremely awkward. I stood up, shook his hand, grabbed Sanjana's and left the office. He operated on Sanjana a few weeks later; he charged her in full and just to annoy him, I carried my Michael Kors to the hospital when I went to visit Sanjana while she recuperated. He didn't really live up to his reputation and Sanjana never went back to him. My trusty Michael Kors accompanies me to every meeting now because no one has the right to judge me by my cover.

19

A Stolen Childhood

> *The magic, the wonder, the mystery and the innocence of a child's heart are the seeds of creativity that will heal the world.*
>
> —Michael Jackson

MY MIND HAD BECOME A DARK PLACE THREE YEARS into Make Love Not Scars, but not the kind of dark you would expect. I felt privileged to know of stories that you wouldn't hear or see on TV or read about in newspapers because they were so grim that the victims refused to share them. I felt privileged, on the one hand, that someone would trust me enough to let me into their lives to such an intimate degree but, on the other hand, it made me sad that because of societal intolerance these stories rarely, if ever, saw the light of day. My mind held all these secrets now and how I wished that I could show the world what was happening. It saddened me that what one actually saw on the news was not even half of what had happened in reality. They didn't get to hear about the long suffering of the victims before the attack. I longed for the day that none of this would happen behind closed doors, a day when a survivor didn't have to conceal the truth about what had happened to them fearing social rejection or stigma.

It is safe to say that by now I had seen more than my fair share of absolutely gruesome burns and gut-wrenching sorrow that would make strong men blench. At times, I caught myself referring to some of the victims in the past tense, as soon as I left the hospital. I instinctively knew that was probably the first and last time I would meet them. I lied as I breezily assured them that they would be just fine.

On 27 December 2016, the universe conspired to teach me a lesson and show me that I hadn't seen the worst yet. I received a call from a lady who worked with the Human Rights Law Network (HRLN) in Delhi informing me about a case that was about ten days old. I was about to board a flight to Delhi from Mumbai (luckily) and was told that the victim was two years old and was finding it hard to receive the treatment that was needed urgently. This case was a perfect fit to receive free treatment so I called Tania and asked her to meet me at the hospital at 11 p.m. which I would reach straight from the airport. She couldn't make it, so my younger sister, Sana, said she would accompany me. The HRLN would also accompany us to help with the legal aspects of the case. On the flight, I struggle to imagine such a small body being so badly brutalised the same way it is hard to fathom how two-year-old toddlers could be raped. When I landed in Delhi, I walked passed the Hamleys toy store and picked up a glove-puppet I somehow imagined would distract the little tyke.

I went straight to the highly-reputed private hospital and as we all converged outside, I saw a frail young man holding what looked like a puppy bundled up in a blanket. It was too dark to see the child's face, but he was whimpering in pain and let out occasional heart-rending cries. Whenever I try to get someone admitted into a private hospital, I do my utmost to maintain business-like objectivity, and not get emotional at all. I avoid looking at or interacting with the victim because when I get emotional, all rationale flies out the window. We walked into the emergency wing entrance with me at the vanguard of the convoy. In my initial discussion with the hospital staff, I don't mention the free-of-cost treatment because they would immediately start thinking up lame excuses to avoid examining the injured little boy. I merely told the nurse that wc had a two-year-old boy who had been burnt with acid and she took us into one of the screened-off cubicles. As soon as the man sat down on the hospital bed with the swaddled child beside him, I hurried off to snare a medic and returned with a doctor in tow. The doctor asked the father to undo the wrapping from his precious bundle. The instant he did, the doctor's blanched in horror, as did I and every single human being in the room that day. His poor little face was dreadfully damaged, pieces of flesh clinging to bones, his agony reflected in his one remaining eye; it felt as heart-breaking as watching all the puppies in the world being slaughtered alive. I had seen burns before but none quite as gruesome; they were infection-infested, puss-oozing, flesh-falling burns, and the worst of it was that they had been inflicted on someone so small and defenceless. I had never seen so much pain, fear and hopelessness in such young eyes. I never knew how physically painful it would be to cry as his salty tears crept into the crevices of his wounds. He was so fragile that the doctor was scared to touch him; but after one look, he said the child was in need of immediate medical intervention.

I was satisfied with this diagnosis because it meant that no one could deny that the child needed immediate hospital admission—the doctor himself had indicated as much. He told me to complete the necessary paperwork and make the relevant payments. I filled out all the forms at the billing counter and instead of payment, I provided them with a copy of the Supreme Court decree which clearly stated that all hospitals (private and national) were legally bound to provide immediate and cost-free treatment. Although this order was crystal clear, the billing desk immediately became reluctant to admit the child. In my head this situation was only too familiar and 'here we go again' was all I thought. This time round however, I was stronger and more assertive, and wasn't about to let anyone brush me aside. The very same doctor who had just informed me about the need for 'immediate medical intervention' returned twenty minutes later and informed us that there was no need for admission. I asked him to give this to me in writing. He refused. I made it very clear that I wouldn't leave unless they admitted him or provided me with a letter that clearly stated that there was no immediate threat to the patient's life and hence he was advised against admission. The doctor tried to convince me that the child's burns were 'thermal' and not the outcome of an acid attack even though he had seemed positive about the acid-attack theory before. I wasn't buying any of it and held my ground.

By broaching the issue, I had already done the heavy lifting and now I left it to the lawyers to argue out the rest. In a relatively peaceful moment, I escaped to the boy's cubicle to give him my glove-puppet. I knew it wouldn't help much, but I thought it was the right thing to do since I had already bought it. To my surprise, the boy's face lit up as I pulled out the puppet and he stopped crying. We were now winning the battle against the salty tears. He seemed to giggle remotely despite the severe injuries around his little lips. This level of brutality was new even for me and against the strict ruling of my modus operandi which forbade my getting an emotional perspective on the cases, I asked his father to tell me what had happened. In most cases, it was a spurned lover attacking a woman. This case had clearly changed the demographics of acid attacks for me and I had to understand why my assumption that these attacks were a form of gender-based violence was suddenly so wrong.

Akash Raj was a happy, fun-loving and goofy two-year old only a fortnight ago. He didn't know how to talk coherently, let alone abuse or offend anyone, however his mother had committed a cardinal sin. She ought to have known better than to have had the audacity to reject the advances of the village goons. She was silly because she thought she had the right to say 'no' without fear of any consequences and although she was ready to deal with the fallout herself, she didn't know that her baby boy would have to pay the price for her ill-judged decision to exercise her fundamental rights. She should have known that, as a woman in India, a 'no' is never really a 'no'.

Akash's mother was harassed for months and although she had complained to her husband, he had advised her to keep mum in fear of getting stigmatised. She did everything she could within her power to stand up for herself. On 12 December, her husband was away on a visit to their native village and she was out on the porch with Akash who suddenly demanded that she buy him some ice cream. She ran upstairs to get some money to fulfil his little heart's desire. She was gone all of five minutes and returned to find her boy missing. She assumed that he had wandered off to play at one of their neighbour's houses as this is common practice in close-knit village communities; she made some casual enquiries in the neighbourhood. When there was no sign of him later in the evening, she filed a complaint at her local police station. Seven months pregnant with her second child, she stayed up all night, riddled with fear, panic and anxiety. She had a bad feeling, but she didn't know what could have happened. The next day, at 8 a.m. she was informed that a little boy's body was found in the dumpster nearby. She ran to the skip and recognised her son by his clothes. When she turned him over to wake him up, she saw his non-existent face and fainted. Akash and his mother lay by the dumpster until a good Samaritan took them both to the hospital. She still remains in a fugue state after this traumatising shock.

I was almost in a trance as Akash's father narrated these terrible events. I had forgotten that we were at the hospital. My spell was broken when Akash lunged forward to grab the hand-puppet that was resting on my thigh. I instantly caught him in my arms and lifted him onto my lap. A thousand questions rampaged through my mind—what the hell was wrong with people in this country? I couldn't understand what special kind of evil one had to possess to brutalise an innocent child in this manner? I could barely articulate my utter loathing for such people.

I handed Akash back to his dad, no longer viewing him as too frail to hold. I marched up to the doctor again and told him I was summoning the police. I didn't listen to his excuses and telephoned the cops who had a van stationed outside the hospital at all times. The constabulary came in and even as I explained my predicament to them, the hospital staff informed me that they would admit Akash until the next morning. I had neither the heart nor courage to say goodbye; I left him in good hands and went home.

As soon as I got home, I started working on a campaign to raise funds for him. Tania sat up all night and drafted the write-up that would go on the campaign page and our crowdfunding partners, Ketto, sat up all night and mobilised the rally. The next day the campaign went live and raised eleven lakhs in two hours. I returned to the hospital to get Akash discharged and transferred to another hospital and to my surprise, the hospital had the nerve to give me a large bill. I said nothing and drove to the police station. While I was there I messaged the medical superintendent of the hospital and told him what I was doing. Five minutes later, he told me that Akash Raj had been discharged free of cost. It was all good and great that the hospital followed the law in that instance but I couldn't stop thinking about the struggle that it had entailed. I couldn't stop thinking about the people that had to do this without my intervention, all the other Akashs who would die in their battle to just get treatment that is rightfully theirs. Treatment that is decreed by the Supreme Court of India, the highest court of law in our country! It was blowing my mind. I was well aware of the situation relating to implementation of laws in my country, I wasn't naïve. But the fact that even a defenceless two-year-old could not invoke enough sympathy in the hearts of big corporate hospitals, that are not only obligated by law but by humanity as well, in order to get treated was mind-boggling.

Akash ended up receiving quality treatment through the funds we raised for him, thanks to all the people that donated towards his campaign. However, it wasn't free treatment as per the law, but no charges were brought against the hospital. His campaign was featured by the *Logical Indian* which was instrumental in helping us raise the funds. Some battles are worth fighting for, but I didn't want a child struck in the crossfire of a legal battle; I just wanted him to get better so I bit my tongue this once. Today, he is much better and thankfully doesn't remember anything because he was too young to process the trauma. His life will never be the same however, and no matter how hard we try, he will never be a pattern card of our society's aesthetic standards. When he grows up, he will wonder why he is treated differently, why the other kids bully him in school and why he does not resemble his younger brother. But I am hoping that we will be around to guide him through those trying times. I hope I can find something as age-appropriate as the glove-puppet that once amused him while I explain to him that this should not make him a bitter human being later in life.

20

Entitled Millennials

FROM THE DAY I DECIDED TO DEDICATE MYSELF TO this cause, I always knew that change was going to be a gradual process. I also believed that if I could understand this, anyone could. I was wrong. I also thought that I would be rich by now; I was wrong again. By this point in my journey, I had won the British Council International Alumni Award (among other prestigious accolades) and had had the great honour of meeting with the Duke and Duchess of Cambridge as well as of Cornwall. The organisation had started receiving funding from Meer Foundation, an organisation run by the king of Bollywood, Shah Rukh Khan. We had managed to streamline processes and had raised over one crore in crowdfunding alone.

From its inception I tried to ensure that Make Love Not Scars gave priority to ideas driven by students and millennials. I believed that if someone had given me a chance when I needed it, I could have cut down my struggle time by half and also preserved some of my self-esteem.

Although I am confident that these hardships helped make me the person I am today, I wanted to let young people be a part of my movement. Today's generation is so driven and passionate that I wanted to help steer them in a direction that would also help make the world a slightly better place. It is amazing what one can do when someone else believes in them. I wanted to believe in other people.

We had reached a stage where we could now actually hire interns, which meant that we could pay them a stipend so they could make it to work and back. It wasn't much but it was definitely more than what other organisations were offering. I didn't want money to be the incentive, but I did realise that passion alone wouldn't pay the bills. It's a different story that my dad was still paying mine, but I like to believe that my sang-froid in the face of the million taunts he threw my way was my contribution towards the household. When we opened up our internship programme, I was overwhelmed by the number of applicants, some of whom seemed even more passionate than I was! Their emails had managed to raise my hopes soaring but after the first few interviews, I fell off cloud-nine and made my way back to reality. I remembered my old friend, the five-minute obligation and almost instantly felt more grounded and started thinking more realistically. The 'five-minute obligation' is a term I invented in college, and it very much applied to me. The concept was simple: give my generation something we should actually care about and we will care about it for all of five minutes. For example, the war in Syria had become a popular five-minute rant during parties and the increasing number of crimes on women was a wine-night favourite amongst the youth. But the question is, even though we spoke about these things for all of five minutes, did we in any way contribute towards bettering the situation? I didn't expect everyone to become overnight activists or launch global campaigns to support the causes that they believed in. At times, even giving a cause the token respect of researching it and then dedicating something as small as a Facebook status to it was a lost idea. My five-minute obligation was broken in college when I found myself thinking about acid attacks for more than two days. Let's also keep in mind that I was going through a tough break-up at the time, that made this thought process even more valued. Call me shallow, but aren't we all?

By the start of the summer, I had managed to recruit five new interns who seemed adequately passionate and hardworking. The centre seemed to be brimming with enthusiasm and I found myself secretly gloating about how I had managed to make social work 'cool'. My interns came from diverse backgrounds; some were as young as sixteen and some were interested in alternative fields like fashion. I say 'alternative' because it goes against the norm of being interested in becoming a lawyer, doctor or engineer in India. I have to admit that I initially believed that having interns would be a lifesaver, it would lighten my workload and we could produce more ground-breaking work than ever before. When this did not happen and I found myself teaching five youngsters how to work, I realised that I had inadvertently taken up the responsibility of mentoring five young adults. I didn't have a problem with this, but it did bother me when some of my interns thought their inherited entitlement meant that they could behave badly.

One morning, I strolled into the centre and one of my lead interns (she was about my age and responsible for keeping the youngsters in check) looked a bit gloomy. I didn't bother to address her mood right away because I wanted to ensure everyone knew what work was assigned to them for the day. While I interacted with the sixteen-year-olds, this particular intern got up and screamed, 'I can't do this!' in a high-pitched voice and stormed out of the room. The other sixteen-year-olds were terrified and I asked myself if I had accidentally asked her to kill someone, when my mind answered: 'obviously not Ria, don't be silly.'

I couldn't understand what had warranted such an absurd outburst. I followed her into the other room where I found her in a flood of tears being consoled by some survivors and assumed there had been a death in her family. I decided to approach the situation with utmost sensitivity and in a calm voice I asked her what had happened. She explained to me how difficult she found it to deal with the lingering effects of sorrow in this line of work. She said all of this in the presence of a survivor. Hey, I'm not a monster, I understand this job is not for everyone, but I'm hoping that when someone comes to work for this cause, they know that we are not in the business of manufacturing teddy bears. I am also hoping that this individual will know better than to rant about their incapacity to deal with sorrow in front of people that have seen the worst of it.

I politely asked the survivors to leave and proceeded to speak to her. I told her that I understood that this line wasn't for everyone and that she shouldn't be so hard on herself and that she was free to leave. She sobbed some more and then got her things together and left.

My sixteen-year-old interns however left a lasting impact on my organisation. Over the next month, on their own initiative they introduced dance classes, reached out to new survivors and hospitals and were the first ones to jump at any and every opportunity to accompany me to the police station. We shall call them enthu-cutlets. Even though I had someone my age, from the same background as I did, she had walked out on a commitment in an unprofessional manner; I learnt that age, truly, is just a number.

Through this journey I have had the honour of working with some great professionals as well as with some millennials with too much of a sense of entitlement. I once had a colleague slack at work, sleep at work and create more work than process it. This colleague, let's call her X, seemed extremely passionate in the beginning, but when she realised that helping people included doing some boring office work, she started losing interest. We were at an important shoot one day and she was extremely late; I called her several times and she made various excuses and I had to speak to her sternly. This did not sit well with her and as soon as she reached the shoot she ripped up at me in front of our sponsors and told me that I couldn't treat her like she was 'low-class'. She proceeded to mention that she came from a noteworthy family and just when she was five seconds away from name dropping, I put an end to it. She slandered me to journalists and even though it made me livid, I realised that this was part and parcel of every work field. Not everyone was going to understand that in order to create a sustainable change, we had to make the survivors independent. I have had employees question why our survivors are not 'rich' yet because they do various ad campaigns, etc., and I have had to explain to them that it's the same reason that I don't get paid a salary. We created campaigns to spread awareness and everyone that worked on them, came on board knowing that they would not get paid for it. I didn't draw a salary because the NGO could never afford it and plus we had made it very clear that we were not going to give survivors money in hand to begin with.

Even though my parents were delighted with the numerous accolades and good karma I was receiving, they always wondered when I would ever be financially independent, and do you know what's funny? This book is the first payment I have ever received for my work. I have had numerous brands and media outlets get in touch for features and I've done most of them but I've never received a penny for them. I have tried to get into the habit of charging for my work, but most brands see fit to pay a model to model their clothes than to pay me to share my story. Everyone believes that just because I run an NGO I should do everything for free—heck, my own government thinks it! As the president of my NGO, I am not allowed to draw salary and never have. As a change-maker and influencer, I am not allowed to ask companies to compensate me for my time either.

This one time, I was approached by a brand, a leading online retailer in women's fashion. Their concept brief was centred around putting change-makers in their designs and using their stories to garner more traction towards their website. This sounded like straightforward product-endorsement to me and when I enquired about what their budget was, they made it very clear that they didn't have one for me. I was truly astonished and retaliated. When I did, they insisted that I wasn't endorsing their clothes and that they just wanted to give me and my cause more publicity ... wearing their outfits. However, since this wasn't an endorsement and their only objective was to help the cause and me, I said I would do the shoot, but in my own clothes. They twigged that I wasn't a fool. Their representative never got back to me and the following month I saw their campaign launch with no known social activists in it.

Similarly, an agency had approached me to star in a campaign for a massive automobiles company. The company wanted to showcase extraordinary Indians that were as powerful as their automobiles (weird but whatever sells, I guess). I told the agency I would charge them and had no doubt that such a large multinational would have no qualms about being ethical. No sooner than I had asked to be paid, the email conversations screeched to a halt. The following month I saw them copy-paste one of my previous interviews as a part of the campaign. Luckily, the company was managed by Ogilvy and since Ogilvy represented us as well, they spoke to them about it. The manufacturers appointed a third person to negotiate and ask me what I wanted. I asked them for a token compensation of one rupee and a public apology. I never received my rupee, but the automobiles company managed to get the PR agency representing them to issue a public apology. I might have seemed like I was making a mountain out of a molehill at the time, but my story and my name was being used to promote a brand without my permission. I don't know about you, but that didn't sit well with me.

It's not just brands. Blogs also make money from the content they put out. So, is it so wrong that I ask for a cut if your content is based on me? I have been approached by numerous blog sites that wanted me to take out three hours of my time and write 5,000-word interviews for them. These are not just interviews though, they are comprehensive essays on my thoughts and articles written by me. The only work the blog has to do is hit the 'publish' button. At the beginning, one takes all the opportunities one can get because one must. I remember spending a lot of my days doing only promotions and writing my story time and time again in different words. One would have thought that I would have learnt to use a thesaurus by now, but I chose to individually give my time to each interview and article. I did long shoots for no one noteworthy, asking for nothing in return, but there comes a point where everyone has to evaluate their own self-worth. I don't believe the time for this evaluation is at the beginning; far from evaluation that would be plain arrogance. It also depends on your portfolio of work and even though mine may not have been humongous, I believe that it had some good stuff in it. I was judging my self-worth through the work I had done for my survivors, so I was basically judging myself through their worth and I believed that I deserved more. This wasn't about me being cocky, this was about me wanting to be compensated for my time. I never asked for this compensation from my own work with the NGO, I did that for free, so I believed that I had the right to make money the same way other people were making money by using my story.

So from where do I get my income? I don't. I live in the hope that one day I'll figure out how to earn enough to not ask my father permission before I buy lingerie, but that day is not today. The year 2016 had seen a rise in the concept of 'activism sells'. Everyone wanted to associate themselves with a cause, with people that were making a change because this is what the audiences wanted to see. Everyone wanted to appear more socially-conscious but they also wanted to do it on a budget. The budget included paying everyone from the camera man, to the director of photography's assistant, but not me. I wanted to put my foot down against this practice, but it wasn't until I read a tweet by my idol Sunitha Krishnan that I actually had the courage to validate my own feelings. She said something along the lines of how everyone wanted her time, but no one wanted to pay her for it, and it really hit home. Just because I was a social activist, did that mean that I would never be able to afford a colour TV or a nice meal out? The concept in my mind was unfair and if anyone deserved to be paid, it was the people that were ensuring a better tomorrow for everyone else's grandchildren. We got into this field to help people but what happens when you cannot even help yourself? Not everyone could afford to do this and no one should have to compromise on his or her dreams of being self-sufficient.

I was clocking in more hours at this point than a regular nine-to-five job. When I wasn't at work, I was on the phone sorting out issues about work. When I wasn't problem-solving, I was counselling survivors on the phone. When I was done counselling the visually-abled survivors, I was counselling the blind ones at night and I don't say all of this to receive any sort of praise, I say all of this because you have to know what you're getting into. When I started, I didn't know that I would have to rely on my parents for every financial necessity and even though I am blessed to have a family that can just about provide for me, I do understand why other people are reluctant to join the social-work sector. This is something that definitely needs to change and in order to convince bright minds to join the field of change-making, we need to be able to offer them decent incentives. But the question remains, how do we provide these incentives when the sector lacks funding even for the ones we are trying to help?

In order to stand by my beliefs, I started to not take part in any brand collaborations without fair payment and guess what? I never did a brand promotion again. It is sad, but it has been worth every bit of it.

#EndAcidSale

On 26 May 2015, I received the following email:

'Hi Ria/ Make Love Not Scars Team,

This is Harshik and Geetanjali. We are working as creatives at O&M, Mumbai—an advertising agency.

At present, we are working on a 'pro bono' campaign on Acid Attack. We hope to meet some of the demands of Acid-Attack Victims—implementation of the ban on the sale of acid in our country. We already have an idea for the campaign, have filmmakers on board and are looking for an NGO partner to take things forward.

We wanted to get in touch with you or a concerned person regarding the same. We can be reached at 097xxxxxxx/099xxxxxxx.

Let us know how we can connect asap.

Thanks,

Geetanjali & Harshik

Creatives

O&M

Mumbai

When I read it, it seemed like just another agency trying to make a quick buck because 'activism sells'. I have to admit, I had no idea who they were or what 'O&M' stood for and because it didn't ring a bell or sound important enough, I didn't even bother googling it. That night, during dinner when my father asked me how work was going, I naturally downplayed it. I spoke about my current cases and casually slipped in the collaboration offer email from O&M in order to sound busy. Almost instantly my father's face lit and up and he said, 'Ri, that's amazing! I hope you replied professionally!' How typical of him to simultaneously give me a compliment and judge my abilities at the same time. Luckily for me I have the gift of selective hearing. I didn't want to sound stupid, so I just mumbled, 'Yeah, of course.' He then went on to talk about O&M and what an honour it was, etc. At this point I could have actually googled it under the table but was caught off-guard when my mouth spoke without my permission and there they were, the dreaded words, 'Dad, what's O&M?' My father's head hung in shame and I felt like I had asked him where babies came from. It also occurred to me at this point that he had caught me lying. Surprisingly, he didn't lose his cool and told me that O&M stood for Ogilvy and Mather (still didn't ring a bell, though). Thank God he proceeded to inform me what they actually did and the minute he said they represent the likes of Google and Rolls Royce, I sprang out of my chair, ran to my room and (almost) calmly started drafting my reply. I didn't want to seem too eager. I drafted a bunch of replies before I realised that none of them were good enough, so I decided to directly call them the next day.

I woke up at exactly 9 a.m. (millennial standard time) and called Harshik, who said that he and his partner would call me back from their conference room in five minutes. It sounded so fancy. Five minutes turned to ten and I was growing impatient to say the least. I wanted this to work out so badly. Fifteen minutes later, my phone rang. I let it ring a couple of times before I picked up because I wanted to seem 'busy' and my time should not be taken for granted. Let's face it though, all I was doing in that moment was waiting for their call. I finally answered the phone and was greeted by two very enthusiastic voices. Harshik had brought along his partner Geetanjali and they started to elaborate on how they were juniors at Ogilvy and had this idea about starting a campaign to end the open sale of acid. Their concept was controversial because it had never been done before and they didn't know if it would come across the way they had planned, but the minute I heard their ideas, I was sold. The more controversial, the better to be honest, innit?

We ended the call on a positive note and they asked me to send them some links of videos that they could go through. They still hadn't confirmed our collaboration at this point and as soon as we hung up, I sent over the few links that we did have. The next few days were modern-day torture. I hadn't heard back from O&M and had started to mourn the loss of a relationship with them (which had never really existed by then). Just when I thought it was all over and the light at the end of the tunnel was about to wink out completely ... there it was. I never knew an email notification could mean as much. I opened it with my fingers crossed.

'Thanks for the videos, Ria.

Some are heart-breaking while some are truly inspiring.

We're really looking forward to work with MLNS on this campaign and make some noise.

Cheers!!

Harshik & Geetanjali'

That was it—I was in. At the age of twenty-two my organisation was going to be represented by the advertising giants, Ogilvy and Mather.

Two months later—

It had now been two whole months since our initial conversation on the campaign. In these two months we had managed to go back and forth on our concept idea, finalise scripts, a director, a production house and now all that was left to do was find the perfect survivors who would be the stars of our campaign. I had sent over pictures of Sapna and Reshma (two completely different cases) to see what they were thinking about. Sapna suffered from mild burns to the left side of her face that stretched slightly above her jaw line and all the way down her arms. The scars were easily concealable with a full-length top and some basic make-up. Reshma on the other hand was into her second-year of recovery and was recovering from over forty per cent burns to her face. To say that she didn't resemble her previous aesthetic would be an understatement. Reshma and Sapna were at opposite ends of the acid-attack spectrum. At this point no one had really seen a full advertising campaign based on an acid-attack survivor or, let's say, no one had seen an entire campaign that brought you face-to-face with devastating disfigurement. I was quite keen on letting the audience know exactly what an acid attack was and the damage it could cause and for that reason among others, I had my heart set on Reshma.

It came as no surprise when the director picked Sapna. He said Reshma was too disfigured—his words not mine. Harshik tried to sugar-coat his words, but the damage was already done. I lashed out at them with the same fury a lioness would have protecting her cubs and I would like to think that I set a precedent because the next day the team decided to pay Reshma a visit before they took a call. I was glad that they would at least consider this, but I knew that they were doing this just to shut me up. Nonetheless, I really didn't mind. I knew Reshma could win anyone over. Reshma, being the timid, docile, well-mannered and coy little girl, reminded me of a child. She never moaned too much but you could see the pain in her eyes. Because she was attacked when she was only seventeen, all her days of experimenting with make-up and clothes like any other teenager were summarily truncated. Reshma was one of my first few cases. I had picked up her case because it hit too close to home. At the age of seventeen, Reshma was attacked by her former brother-in-law. Reshma's older sister, Gulshan, was married to a man who often beat her up, threw her out of the house and cursed her for having given birth to a girl even though she had subsequently given birth to a boy. A couple of months before the attack, her husband kidnapped their baby boy after Gulshan dared to leave him for the last time. As any other desperate mother would, Gulshan filed a complaint against her husband and the police had ordered that the child be returned. The vindictive man plotted to ruin his wife's life. At 8 a.m. that day, Reshma and Gulshan decided to swap their burkhas for a change. They had no clue that such an innocuous wardrobe decision would come with such a heavy price. Just as they arrived at the train station to travel to the nearby town, two men on a motorbike stopped them. When Gulshan realised who the men were, she told Reshma to run. Reshma ran, but the hoodlums caught up with her, pinned her to the ground and one of the men who happened to be her brother-in-law, doused her face with acid. She was attacked for no reason, a senseless crime based on the lack of value for human life, an Indian woman's life. A crime based on the arrogance of impunity. Reshma and I had created a solid bond by now and I had become her 2 a.m. suicide call. I had managed to talk her out every time though.

The reason I picked Reshma was because she was different from the other girls. The other girls seemed to have given up on their appearances after their attack. They stopped putting on make-up, wearing nice clothes and refused to get all dolled up but Reshma wanted to make the best of a grim situation. It started with just a little bit of *kohl* on her one remaining eye and before we knew it she was using the wrong shade of foundation—but it was foundation nonetheless, a common mistake made by all girls dabbling in make-up. I could tell she would eventually shine, but at the end of the day, it didn't matter what I thought, everyone had to agree.

I wasn't in Mumbai when the team went to meet Reshma and I'm not quite sure what transpired. All I do know is that the team saw in Reshma exactly what I wished they had at the outset. They were all converts now. Everyone agreed that casting Reshma was the right thing to do because it represented the cause well but, at the same time, they unanimously believed that it was a risk. Our audience would either look away or they would look deep and we decided that it was our responsibility to ensure that they didn't look away. The content had to be so powerful that Reshma became both the vessel of the message as well its crusader. The idea was simple, we were going to create three viral make-up tutorials which would feature Reshma teaching her followers how to apply different types of make-up. We were going to make her a beauty Vlogger, we just didn't know at this time that she would forever be etched into history.

Reshma would end each video with a call to action and our call to action was to sign a petition that we were to write, addressed to the prime minister of India to get him to implement the ban on the open sale of acid. India is a funny place you see, we pass laws for fun. The second there is an uprising, a mini-revolution, enough noise to shake the system, a new law is born. This law is meant to serve as a pacifier to show the public that the government and the judiciary care. They create these over-ambitious laws with no plans on how to implement them and girls like Reshma end up becoming the silent examples of its failures.

In 2013, the Supreme Court of India had directed all Indian states to ban the open sale of acid (over the counter), which meant that there would finally be some sort of accountability for where all this acid was coming from. This would also mean that acid would become hard to procure hence bringing down the rate of acid attacks altogether. If Indian states had actually listened to this and implemented this law, Reshma might have not been the star of this campaign today. The state heads were to reconvene in a month's time from the day the order was passed to submit a concrete action plan of how this would be implemented and ... guess what? No meeting. No such meeting ever took place. No plans were submitted. No action was taken and hence #EndAcidSale was born.

As soon as Reshma was finalised for the campaign, a shoot date was set for the following week and we all sprang into action. Since this campaign was the brainchild of two juniors and not someone higher up at Ogilvy, we literally had no budget. Even though Harshik and Geetanjali's immediate bosses, Harshad and Kainaz were always supportive. Everyone who volunteered to work on this campaign did it only for the cause. It is possible that some people did it for credit and bragging rights as well, but not everyone was like that. The people who actually mattered and were going to drive this campaign, were doing it for the right reasons and that was all that mattered. I flew to Mumbai a day before the shoot. We were going to meet at the studio at sharp 9 a.m., because shooting three videos in one day was going to be a Herculean task and we didn't have the budget to even rent out the studio for an extra day. Harshik, Geetanjali and I converged at the studio at about the same time and were astonished to see that the set hadn't even been put up by then. Since we were not paying for anything really, we quickly realised that huffing and puffing would be wholly futile. Instead we galvanised ourselves into action. Harshik and Geetanjali ran to a props store to rent out objects that one would normally find in a seventeen-year-old's bedroom and I helped by encouraging the set design team to start painting the pink walls for the background. By 'encouraging' I really mean chivvying them along in my sweetest voice; you really can catch more bees with honey than with vinegar, especially when you are on a shoestring budget. As I used my flirting skills to my advantage and Harshik and Geetanjali ran around town, the production team arrived with all the hustle and bustle of a large-scale shoot. H & G soon got back with all the pretty little gewgaws that one would find in a girly bedroom, some fairy lights and lots of overall sparkle.

The production team had started to set up cameras and the set was finally coming together. The background had been painted pink and all the little frames and lights were strung on them. Reshma had arrived and had already been put into her first look. She was handed the script and went through it while the hair and make-up team glammed her up. I caught myself looking at her for a moment with nothing but pride and couldn't believe how far she had come. She was visibly nervous because she had never done anything like this before, but I could tell she was super excited as well. I had asked a friend of mine who also happened be a Bollywood actress, to come and help Reshma with her lines and Amyra did not disappoint with her enthusiasm. Amyra guided Reshma through the script and helped her with facial expressions while the rest of us scrambled to put the finishing touches on the set and create the perfect frame that matched the director's standard of perfection. When everything was ready and Reshma was placed in front of the camera, everyone stopped breathing for a second. She was truly beautiful. It was a surreal moment as everyone gasped at the gravity of what we were trying to pull off. We had done it. This was where she was destined to be and we were the privileged spectators.

Shooting the first video took longer than we had thought and before we knew it, half the day was over. We decided that we really needed to speed up the process.

Reshma was having trouble pronouncing some of the words so we decided that we would correct that through voice-over recordings later on in order to get on with the day. As soon as we arrived at this decision, the shoot went on faster. It was 9 p.m. now and we still hadn't finished the third and final video. Reshma was exhausted and the rest of us were pretending not to be in order to keep up her morale. At 11 p.m. we finally wrapped up and as soon as we were done, everyone broke into huge cheers and hoorays for this beautiful girl's dedication. It had been an exhausting, emotionally-draining and rough day for all of us but we all felt honoured to have been able to do this. You could feel it in the air, we had created something of substance. We felt the magic because we were there, but was our audience going to feel it too? Had we indeed crossed the line and shot something that someone wouldn't want to see? A lot was on the line, but for me, the only thing that I was worried about was Reshma's feelings. I was worried that if she didn't get received properly she would be scarred a second time over and my conscience couldn't afford that; I had, after all, bulldozed everyone into casting her.

The shoot may have been over, but I still had tonnes of work to do where the backend work was concerned. The *Logical Indian*, which is one of India's biggest social media news pages, came on board as media partners which ensured that when we released our campaign, it would have a guaranteed viewership. Bharat who was one of the website's founding members and a dedicated Make Love Not Scars volunteer and supporter, was put in charge of creating the petition that would be put on the website and because he worked with the *Logical Indian* and us, he was also in charge of creating the flowsheet for the campaign. The flowsheet would include the release dates and times based on social media research. Ensuring that our website looked immaculate and creating a separate page-front for the campaign was Ady's (Aditya) responsibility. Ady had been working with us for two years now and did all our website upkeep free of cost which already made him amazing to me. The next two months consisted of quarrels and squabbles between Ogilvy and Ady's teams, fights between me and Bharat on differences of opinions where our headlines were concerned and it was clear to see that everyone was on edge. At this point, I was working out of my living room and my mother could see that I was extremely stressed; my maid would pacify me with umpteen cups of coffee which in turn could have been the sole reason that I was so wired. After two long months of ensuring everything was spotless or as spotless as it could be, I got on a call with H & G. H was a visionary and working with one could be the best thing you do but could also prove to be extremely annoying. He never thought we were ready to launch because 'one word was off' here and there or the 'vibe' didn't feel right. I was creative too but this was truly another level of mental creative torture that I could not comprehend, so I finally put my foot down.

I told them we were to launch tomorrow. H tried to be diplomatic, but as he started to say, 'Don't you think we should wait another da—' I put a full stop to it. I went down the emotional blackmail route and said, 'You gotta trust me, bro.' Now that I think of it, he had absolutely no reason to 'trust me' because I had no background whatsoever in any of this and was a decade his junior in age. Fortunately and unfortunately, he said 'yes' and I was quick to hang up and call Bharat to give him the green light. I called Bharat at 6 p.m. to tell him to hit the 'publish' button on the first article that contained the first video at 8 p.m. sharp. He wasn't convinced either but I just wanted to get this over and done with and to be honest, I had immense faith in what we had created. Now if this flopped, everyone had only one person to blame, me.

21

#EndAcidSale

HUMANS ARE BORN WITH A NEED TO CONTROL THINGS that are important to them, which is why they fear change and time. We fear things which we cannot control, not realising that if it's meant to be, it will be. Although this notion really doesn't apply if you haven't put in the work, like saying, 'Don't bother studying for that exam. If you're meant to get 90 per cent, then you will get 90 per cent.' LOL, hell no! That's not how it works.

None of us had anticipated what would happen when #EndAcidSale went live. The concept was far too new and had never been tested. I know I had been confident when I said we should just go ahead and launch it, but at about 7.30 p.m., I started having second thoughts. My gut instinct told me it was the right thing to do, but on the other hand, I was scared that it would fail. But then again, I thought to myself, 'How can it? Reshma is in it.' I had so much confidence in the survivors that with that last question, I decided to stop worrying and call it a night.

We had put in the work and now it was time to let destiny do its thing.

I promised myself that as soon as the video went live I wouldn't keep refreshing it to see how many hits we got. However, promises are obviously meant to be broken, so there I was, finger on the button, ready to refresh the video page every couple of minutes. 8.00 p.m., no post on the *Logical Indian* page. 8.01 p.m., no post. 8.02 p.m., no post. 8.03 p.m., and there it was '...'

At this point, I should have called H or G so we could witness together what was to happen next, but I really didn't think about it much. I knew that we would have some views, I mean that is the whole point of launching on a page with a massive following, but by 11 p.m., Reshma's video had 500,000 views. We had decided that when we hit 25,000 signatures on our petition, we would be satisfied. That night we had hit 50,000 signatures. Reshma was making advertising history. None of us could believe what was happening and by now we were calling each other and not really saying anything. We just found comfort in being speechless together. It was really happening; the world was responding to our passion project. I sat stunned as I saw the emails pour in. Emails of support and so many media requests that I knew we possibly couldn't do them all. The *Wall Street Journal*, *People Magazine*, *Marie Claire*, *Time Magazine* and every other publication in every other field.

I had spent the entire night responding to media requests, comments and queries. I had never seen shit hit the fan like this (in a good way, of course). Things were moving at lightning speed and the next morning the entire team was chipping in. Bharat did a couple of interviews, H & G picked up a few, but Reshma was the one doing all the heavy lifting. Reshma was in and out of interviews all day long and I was playing the manager, setting up interviews, prioritising publications, handling our booming inbox and coordinating Reshma's schedules. EVERYONE wanted to speak to Reshma. H & G met up with Reshma in Mumbai and briefed her about what to say since this was Reshma's first actual brush with a media storm. None of us really had the chance to speak to each other about the success of this campaign because we were too busy trying to ensure that Reshma's voice reached every corner of the world. The first couple of days were identical, the buzz really didn't die down. We were all running on minimal sleep and lots of coffee.

One week into the campaign, and we had released all three videos. Reshma was now being invited to grace events, speak publicly about her advocacy, appear on TV and that was when we decided to take it to the next level. On an urgent basis, we shot a new ad campaign and plastered it on billboards all over Mumbai. It was clear that Reshma had a message and it was now becoming hard to ignore her. She had made her point, India had a debilitating problem with acid attacks.

The day when the first billboard came up, Reshma and her family went to the site. Reshma stood under the great hoarding of her face and admired it in awe. She then burst into tears and called me. She told me I had helped her find herself again; the world respected her because of me. If I had known that all it would take was a billboard to show this girl what she was worth, I would have done it a year ago, but I guess everything happens in good time for a reason.

Six months into the campaign, and the buzz still hadn't died down. We were now at 300,000 signatures and Reshma was flying to various cities in India and spreading her advocacy on various prestigious platforms. The campaign was winning Ogilvy every advertising award there was to be won and the two juniors in whom no one had believed at the time, except their immediate bosses, Kainaz and Harshad, were finally being acknowledged as powerhouses of talent. The campaign went on to bag the three Cannes Lions, the most memorable one being the Gold Lion in Film which no Indian agency had won in eight years. We brought it home. Reshma and I couldn't physically be in Cannes to accept it so the Ogilvy team collected the award on our behalf; H held up his phone to the camera and as I saw the show live on my computer from India, I teared up when the camera zoomed in on a picture of Reshma and me. I broke down as my parents hugged me. We were definitely there in spirit.

Soon after, I received an email from a company called FTL Moda in collaboration with a charity called Global Disability Inclusion. The email said they wanted to fly

Reshma down to New York to walk the ramp at New York Fashion Week. I was in complete shock. I quickly called up the team and let them know. I called everyone but Reshma.

I invited Reshma to my mother's house in Mumbai and decided to record her reaction as I told her. I sat her down and showed her pictures of various parts of New York and tried to get her to guess which city I was hinting at. The video was a fail because she kept saying 'Dubai' and I realised how ignorant I was for quizzing her like this considering she had never set foot outside this country. I finally revealed that she would be going to 'America' and that got the tears flowing. The video went viral and we were on our way to New York a few months later. This didn't come without its fair share of hiccups over passports and visas, but let that be a story for another time.

Reshma and I were not flying together to America. Reshma would be winging her way solo, so I made little notes that she could hand over to ground staff, immigration officers, the air hostesses and stewards in case she needed help. I reached a few hours early and was at the airport to pick her up along with the documentary crew that was to film her story from the instant she landed. A tired Reshma was one of the last passengers to emerge. As soon as I saw her, I ran up to her and thought in my mind 'we made it'. We went straight to the hotel and slept like babies.

The next day was back-to-back press interviews with every channel on the face of this planet. I was put in charge of translating for Reshma. By the time we reached the last couple of interviews, the journalist would ask her a question and she would tell me in Hindi that she was dog tired. I had all her answers memorised anyway so I just answered on her behalf without bothering to even ask her by the end of it. She was having a parallel conversation with me in Hindi all the while as I answered the media's questions to her in English. It's sad but quite funny that the journalists weren't aware that she was actually talking about what she wanted to have for dinner later, as I translated that into how horrific it was being attacked with acid. They were deeply moved and Reshma, who found it hysterical, couldn't help chuckling; the journalists probably thought it was a coping mechanism, so they would laugh along politely. Being the only person who knew exactly what was happening in that room, I can say it was hilarious. After a full day of work, we met up with my best friend from school, Anaaya, whose father was currently working in New York.

Anaaya took us to a restaurant close by and witnessed the awesome speed with which we devoured our food. The three of us headed back to the hotel to prepare for the 'walk' the next day. We woke up at 6 a.m. and reached the venue on time. Between hair, make-up, media and fittings, we were coaching Reshma on how to walk. The second Reshma sat down to get her make-up done, the media swarmed the table and all we could see were flashing lights, they were only there to see Reshma walk. Reshma was going to open the show. When the show was about to start,

Reshma held on to my hand and wouldn't let go; she was rightfully nervous. When someone from the team came to get her, I gave her a hug and let go of her hand; it was time to watch her fly. Reshma set the ball rolling for the show and everyone gasped and clapped, the media went crazy. I don't think any of us had registered the enormity of this moment, we were just exhausted and wanted to head back to our hotel to sleep. We woke up the next morning to the whole world talking about Reshma. I had missed calls from Indian journalists, emails from others and woke up to find her face in the newspaper. It was surreal.

That is where Reshma's journey started; she went on to visit various countries like Lebanon to give interviews and was on the cover of *NewsWeek* magazine in the Middle East. Her memoir was released just a month before this book; it was written by Tania. What a funny full circle everything comes to.

22

The Higher You Soar, the Further You Fall

2017 HAD PROVED TO BE AN AMAZING YEAR. SOMETIME in August, I had received a call from someone very special. Her name was Tracey, Tracey Seaward. Tracey had visited the Make Love Not Scars rehabilitation centre in 2016 with her friend and colleague Beeban Kidron. The day I was contacted by their team to plan their visit, I was ecstatic. Like any die-hard *Queen* and *Bridget Jones Diary* fan, I am well aware that Tracey, an extremely well-established and inspiring producer, and Beeban, directed the *Bridget Jones Diary* series. They were in India researching an upcoming project and I was thrilled to have them come over and meet the survivors. It was a day I never forgot.

I was pleasantly surprised to receive a call from Tracey in August but didn't know the context of it. She only said that she needed to speak to me about something. When we got on the call, she told me about an award ceremony that takes place in New York which is organised by UNICEF and the Bill and Melinda Gates Foundation. As she explained it to me in detail, I could sense a great opportunity for a collaboration coming on. The sheer enormity of this event had me excited. She told me about Yusra Mardini who had won the award last year and I remember being a fan of hers when I saw her inaugurate the Olympics for the refugee team. I was in awe of Yusra's story from the moment I heard it. While I was busy daydreaming on the phone about Yusra, Tracey politely and calmly slipped in these words, 'Yeah, so Yusra won it last year and I'm calling you today to let you know that they've decided to give it to you this year.' I swear I almost fainted for a second when I heard this and then burst into frantic tears as Tracey congratulated me. I later found out that she had nominated me. I don't think I could ever thank her enough.

I flew to New York in September and the month before my departure consisted of hours of practice with my life coach, Viraj. Viraj had really proved to be a life-saver at this point. My anxiety was at its peak, but I was oddly excited at the same time. I had to make a two-minute acceptance speech at the ceremony and thanks to Viraj, I actually felt prepared for the first time in my life, that is until the actual night of the awards. My mom accompanied me to New York and my sister Sana, who was studying in California at the time, flew down for moral support as well. The award I was receiving was called the Goalkeeper Award and I was to win under the category 'leadership'. On the day of the awards, I, along with the other winners, got to visit the UNICEF headquarters which was an amazing experience. We ran slightly late there and had to rush back to the hotel to get ready for the ceremony. My hands shook as I took a shower and got my make-up on and it was so rushed that I barely remember any of it.

The awards were held in a beautiful, high-ceilinged, vintage hall. The moment I walked in, I was assigned someone who would help me with my PR and take me in for all the various interviews I had to give. I was ushered from room to room giving interviews while my mom and Sana acted like doting cheerleaders, held my bag and provided words of wisdom between all the moving around. The moment I found out that I was to be seated on the same table as Melinda Gates, Will.i.am and Priyanka Chopra (who was presenting me with the award) amongst other distinguished guests, I felt the onset of a panic attack. I was desperately trying to keep it together, but seemed to be failing spectacularly.

In the end however, it turned out all right because I got to spend the evening discussing leadership and change with Mrs Gates, received a pep talk from Priyanka Chopra and had the honour of witnessing Will.i.am call my mother 'mumma Sharma' when she asked him for a selfie. I didn't have the heart to ruin the moment and explain that that wasn't her last name anymore. She didn't seem to mind either and to be honest I think he could have called her anything and she would have melted. I gave my two-minute address during which I barely looked at the audience, but the silver lining was that I didn't faint. All in all, it was a night to remember.

The next day was the Goalkeepers event which was a day-long conference like none other. I heard Malala, Justin Trudeau, Bill Gates and President Obama speak to name a few. It was safe to say that I was so inspired that I felt like I could truly change the world. Nothing however prepared me for what was about to happen next. I was asked to meet in the lobby for a 'VIP' photoshoot but was never told who it was going to be with. As soon as I reached the lobby, the UNICEF representative told me and the four other girls who had been chosen for this shoot that we were about to meet President Obama. We stood still and eyed each other before breaking into laughter and cheers. It was like we had collectively won the Oscars. We were escorted backstage, our phones were taken away and we were given special security badges. We waited anxiously as we were told 'it' would happen in a couple of minutes. There was a whole lot of nail-biting involved. Really, no one prepares you for the moment you are about to meet your idol. A man whose words have resonated within your very soul, what was I going to say? Was I going to make a fool of myself? Oh well, whatever it was, I was trembling, and I couldn't believe my lucky stars. Just when I thought I would have a few more minutes to prepare myself, an entourage of security emerged and behind them President

Obama walked, chatting with Mrs and Mr Gates. My heart stopped.

President Obama took a good two minutes talking to each of the four of us; I was the last and my nerves were pretty shredded. Then it happened, he walked over to me and I died and went to heaven. He shook my hand and I gushed, 'Thank you so much for changing the world, Mr President'. YES, of all the things I could have said, that's what actually came out. He replied, 'No, it's YOU who's changing the world,' and I hotly disclaimed his praise with, 'No ... No ... It's YOU!' I wish I had something more inspiring to tell you really, but that's what I did with my once-in-a-lifetime opportunity. He then told me he had read about my work and was very impressed and that he planned to be in India in the next couple of months to launch the Obama Foundation and would love to have me there. I didn't know how to tell him that I'd show up regardless of an invite but appreciated how the invite would make me look less stalker-ish. We then got a picture together and I proceeded back to the lobby where I sat in silence trying to make sense of what just happened. The reality truly sank in when Sana found it harder to believe than I did. It sank in when mom's shrieks pierced through the phone because she wasn't at the event. It sank in when my father almost passed out on the long-distance call and became all the more real when I received the pictures a few days later.

2017 was really proving to be the best year of my life ... until we hit November. At this point, Make Love Not Scars was thriving; we were receiving tonnes of support and it seemed like nothing could stop us. I had just happened to receive a new case one fine morning—her name was Zakira. She was attacked by her husband on the basis of a groundless suspicion of infidelity and was currently fighting for her life at a hospital in Mumbai. I hadn't met her but had received pictures from the hospital where she was. The hospital had asked for help so I sprang into action that very day and set up a crowdfunding campaign for her. She had some of the worst burns I had ever seen and I knew that if we didn't raise the money, she would end up in a government hospital where she wouldn't stand a chance. She would need twenty-five lakhs according to the hospital's estimate. Five days into running the campaign, we had managed to raise a significant sum of eleven lakhs and that's when I started receiving threatening calls and messages from an NGO based in Mumbai. This NGO was run by a survivor herself who claimed that this was 'her case' and that I should back off. I made it very clear that I didn't want any credit for my contribution and that I just wanted to help. She evidently felt threatened and refused my offer. She then proceeded to poison Zakira's family against me by telling them that I was raising funds on their behalf and had no intention of giving them the money. MLNS had a very clear policy that the funds raised would directly be transferred to the hospital account in order to avoid misuse. The morning that I decided to end the campaign, I had received a message from this competing

NGO threatening to ruin my credibility. I decided to end the campaign and asked the crowdfunding website to initiate the fund transfer. In the meanwhile, however, the other NGO had come through on their threats and used a tabloid newspaper to run an eight-article long smear-campaign against me. One would think they would stop there, but it was like the NGO had brainwashed the newspaper and they wouldn't listen to a word I said and refused to take into account any of the evidence I provided. The articles were released between the months of November through to the first week of January 2018. They resulted in two false cases against me.

The police said that an FIR had to be filed because they were being pressurised and in the process, my family suffered tremendously. I had to sit with the police officials for over two days to record my statement and simultaneously deal with the bad press. I would often wake up in cold sweat fearing that another piece might have been published while I was asleep, ending up with another sleepless night. I was evidently distraught and it started taking a toll on my mental health. Through this journey, I never once released a public statement because my lawyers believed it would hamper the police investigation. The final blow came on the day when the corporate that funded our centre suspended their partnership with us due to the false allegations. I tried to reason with them, but I realised how bad it all looked. That's when I decided to take matters into my own hands. I put up a lengthy Facebook statement with all the evidence that the newspapers didn't publish regardless of my many attempts and pleas to make them. The Facebook post started garnering a lot of support online which ended with the newspaper calling me up and requesting a meeting. The meeting took place a couple of days after I put up the post and resulted in absolutely nothing substantial. They didn't have much to say but the good thing that came out of this was that they stopped publishing about me. I think they realised that there was some truth in what I was saying, otherwise they wouldn't have stopped. They also understood that I was no longer willing to take things lying down and was ready to fight for my rights.

By the end of February 2018, I was still reeling from everything that had transpired and I was exhausted. We were strapped for funds that the survivors depended on and until the police filed their closure report, my reputation was dwindling. March brought with it some good news however. I had woken up to find myself on the Forbes 30 under 30 Asia list and it was just the sort of validation I needed to make myself believe that I wasn't the most-hated person on the planet. That's the thing, though, when something bad happens to us we often believe that the whole world hates us. We don't realise that just because our lives are at a standstill doesn't mean that the world has stopped moving as well. The recognition from Forbes helped me believe that my career wasn't over. In May, the police finally filed my closure report in court stating that not only was I found innocent by their investigation but that I was also maliciously and falsely indicted. The report came as a much-needed respite and nothing gave me more joy than forwarding it to all our funders. After a rough couple of months, things were finally looking up!

I was sitting at the centre one sunny July afternoon when the landline rang. I barely ever pick up the landline but as fate would have it, no one else was around that day. As I picked up the phone a timid voice on the other line said, 'Ria, ma'am?' I said 'yes' and the voice replied, '*Mein* Zakira.' I almost had a heart attack. I never thought I would have the opportunity to speak to a survivor who had triggered so much upheaval. I was delighted to hear her voice because I never had the chance to even ask her how she was doing or say hello. It was a pleasant surprise and a long conversation during which she explained that she had no control over what happened and had been brainwashed by the other NGO. I told her that I didn't hold anything against her and that she shouldn't worry about anything but getting better. She was in dire need of help and medical intervention. Ever since she was discharged from the hospital six months ago, the other NGO hadn't facilitated even one surgery for her. They didn't so much as help her support her two children. Without a second thought, I told her to visit the centre in Delhi; she agreed without hesitation. Everyone around me was sceptical and asked me how I could trust her so easily; but I knew that someone who had gone through so much already and still needed help was not going to be vindictive. My mind was made up, I was going to help Zakira again. Even though the last time I attempted to do this I was brought down, I made peace with the notion that this kind of thing came with the territory.

Zakira stayed at the centre for all of three days. During her sojourn with us, I got quite comfortable with her and she opened up about how she had been attacked by her husband. She claimed that her husband was always jealous of her passion to want to make something of herself. He would be suspicious of her work or if she put on lipstick, but Zakira was quite the feisty cookie. She fought right back. She wanted to give her two daughters a better life and that served to be her driving force. She also told me about how in a weird way she was happy that this happened to her because even though it left her permanently scarred and disabled, it still ensured that her husband no longer had any say in her life and her daughters'. I was moved to tears to hear this and pledged to help her move on. Zakira was to return to Mumbai and come back to Delhi the following month to start her medical procedures. The first procedure was the most important one, an attempt to save her remaining eye. As Zakira journeyed back to Mumbai, she had several long telephone conversations with me and told me that the other NGO was now threatening her and poisoning her against me. However, Zakira and I had managed to create a bond that I knew was going to withstand the test of time. It was going to take more than just courage to stand up to these people, but Zakira was ready for the uphill battle. Zakira's family was not supportive either and had no qualms about telling her that it would have been a whole lot better if she had died because they believed, given her level of disfigurement, she would never lead a normal life again. I was convinced that she was going to prove them wrong one day. Zakira flew back to Delhi the following month, underwent her first procedure and is all set to make a speedy recovery. On some level I wish I had met her sooner and none of the drama had transpired; I'm not saying that because it would have saved me trouble. I believe that if I had met her sooner, I could have started work on her recovery sooner. I could have ensured that by now she was significantly better, but I guess everything happens for a reason. I had faced my first major setback and realised how it was all a blessing in disguise. I also realised how much work it took to make a reputation and how fast and easily it was tarnished. I learnt that sometimes it's not enough to say that you are passionate about something, you have to learn to fight for the things you love. I fought for Make Love Not Scars with every ounce of strength I had for those months and in the end, I was blessed with another friend, Zakira.

Acknowledgements

My grandparents

My Mamawa, thank you for always watching over me from wherever you are.

My Dada, my voice of reason, my sounding board.

My Granny, my soap opera queen.

My Dadi, my second mother, my definition of love.

My parents

My mother, the more I write about you, the more you'll lose your value (I refuse to share you). Without you there is no me, Katie. My biggest achievement will always be being your daughter.

My father, Dad, you have my heart. I love you more than you will ever know. I hope this book helps you see that I'll be okay in life...even if I don't get married.

My stepmother, Mon, thank you for being such a blessing in my life.

The love of my life

Chooch,
'Out beyond ideas of wrongdoing
and rightdoing there is a field.
I'll meet you there.
When the soul lies down in that grass
the world is too full to talk about.'

My sisters

Meher, you are a beautiful person. I love you for all the things you do for everyone around you. I am lucky to have you in my life not only because of you but because you brought Sameer along. It's safe to say I'd be lost without you.

Sana, you are my sunshine on a rainy day. I am so proud of the strong, independent woman you have become.

Tania

My best friend, the CEO of Make Love Not Scars, and the only person who gets my soul. I love you, Tan, you have saved me time and time again and I'll never be able to repay you. You instil my faith in humanity when I don't seem to believe and I hope everyone is as privileged as me to have a friend like you. You are a superior being and as close to perfection as anyone can get.

My family

Rajat Tauji, Tinku Taiji.

Rakhi Bua, Sameer uncle.

Rita Masi, you more than anyone else, have been there through the journey of writing this book. You have heard me out in time of need, you have advised me on this book and have been instrumental in guiding me.

I cannot thank you enough for all that you've done.

My best friends

Anaaya, you will always be my north star, my way back home.

Misha, without you the centre wouldn't exist and I would be incomplete.

Gayatri, not only are you responsible for the make-up on this cover and how amazing it makes us all look but you are also one of the most genuine people I have ever had the honour of coming across.

Amritah, Raghav, Jyotsana, Vikram, Karan, Anshul, Ishaan, Ayush. Soooshi (Sushant), Sanya, David, you all continue to keep me strong on days when I want to give up.

The backbone of this book

Kanishka, K, you are the reason I have the privilege of typing all this right now. Thank you for having faith in me.

Chandrima, you are a magician. I should have left it at that but you, more than anyone else, knows how much I ramble. I cannot thank you enough for helping me with this book. You are an angel.

Vinit, you have always helped us. Having this cover shot by you has made my heart whole. You will never know just how much you mean to me.

Harshik, I don't even know what to say about you. I will never be able to put in words what place you hold in my life.

Harshad, I can't thank you enough for the amount of time you have spent designing this cover, asking for nothing in return. Regardless, thank you, H. We did it!

Debasri, I write these words because you believed.

Bharat, you haven't been a part of this book but it is because of you that I have been able to write it. You believed in me when no one else did, even though I have had to hound you. B, all words fail me when I talk about everything that you taught me. You are mentioned here because I want to thank you for the contribution you have made towards me, MLNS and all the other things you silently work on to make the world a better place.

Arshia Mehta, for helping with the cover.

Shaheen, you have taught me more than I can ever dream of learning. I cannot thank you enough.

Geetika, you have supported MLNS in times of adversity. I will never be able to express my gratitude enough. Meer Foundation is truly an integral part of MLNS.

Ashish, the MLNS Rehab Centre runs because you believe in it. Thank you.

Haseena, you will always be the reason all this began.

Vidur Kapur and Tarini Manchanda, for so generously helping me bring my vision to life.

Keshav Suri, for always being so supportive of MLNS.

Pathways World School, for not only encouraging me as an individual always but MLNS as well.

The British Council, for their support.